THE

B⬤B™

BOOK

To The Best Bob
EVER! ☺

♡ — your Favorite
cousin
— Jean

THE

B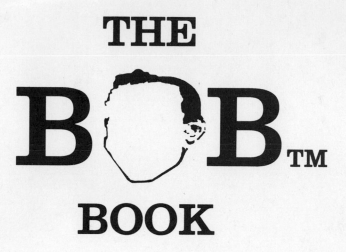B™

BOOK

A CELEBRATION OF THE ULTIMATE
OKAY GUY

BY

DAVID RENSIN AND BILL ZEHME

A Dell Trade Paperback

For Suzie & Emmett.—DR
For my dad, Bob.—BZ

A DELL TRADE PAPERBACK

Published by
Dell Publishing
a division of
Bantam Doubleday Dell Publishing Group, Inc.
666 Fifth Avenue
New York, New York 10103

ISBN: 0-440-50312-4

Printed in the United States of America

Published simultaneously in Canada

June 1991

10 9 8 7 6 5 4 3 2 1

Produced by: 2M Communications
Designed by: Kay Schuckhart

INTRODUCTION
by Bob Greene

PART ONE: THE MEANING OF BOB

GARRISON KEILLOR'S LAKE WOBEGON BOBS: BOB'S BANK; **DINOSAUR BOB** by William Joyce; **LOUD BOB** by Ellen Meloy; **PAR FOR BOB TWAY** by Peter de Jonghe; **THE END OF BOB'S BOB HOUSE** by Ian Frazier; **DAVID LYNCH ON BOB'S BIG BOY**; **GARRISON KEILLOR'S LAKE WOBEGON BOBS: BOBISM**

PART TWO: THE WORLD ACCORDING TO BOB

PART THREE: THE CELEBRATED BOB

BOB BARKER, game-show host; **BUFFALO BOB SMITH,** Howdy Doody's pal; **BOB COSTAS,** sportscaster; **BOB CUMMINGS,** actor; **BOB DENVER,** actor; **BOB DOLE,** Republican senator from Kansas; **BOB DYLAN,** musician; **BOB EINSTEIN,** actor: "Super Dave Osborne"; **BOB ELLIOT,** comedian: Bob and Ray; **BOB EUBANKS,** game-show host; **BOB EVANS,** founder of Bob Evans Farms; **BOB FELLER,** pitching legend; **BOB GOEN,** game-show host; **ROBERT "BOB" GOULET,** entertainer; **BOB GUCCIONE, JR.,** editor/publisher, *Spin* magazine; **BOB HOPE,** entertainer; **BOB KANE,** creator of Batman; **BOB KEESHAN,** Captain Kangaroo/child advocate; **BOB MACKIE,** designer; **BOB MARTWICK,** Morris the Cat's owner/handler; **BOB McGRATH,** *Sesame Street* regular; **BOB MILLER,** governor of Nevada; **BOB NEWHART,** comedian; **BOB RICHARDS,** Olympic champion; **BOB SAGET,** comedian/actor; **ROBERT "BOB" URICH,** actor; **BOB VILA,** builder/TV host; **BOB WEATHERWAX,** Lassie's owner/trainer; **BOB WELCH,** Oakland A's pitcher

Bob BALABAN, actor/film director; **Bob BALDWIN,** jazz keyboard artist; **Bob BELL,** former Bozo; **Bob BODEN,** director ABC-TV daytime development; **Bob BOOKMAN,** Hollywood agent; **Bob BROWN,** editor/publisher, *Soldier of Fortune* magazine; **Robert "Bob" CHRISTGAU,** *Village Voice* rock critic; **Bob COLACELLO,** contributing editor, *Vanity Fair* ; **Bob DOVE,** consultant to Republican Senate leader; **Bob EZRIN,** record producer; **Bob FALLS,** artistic director of Chicago's Goodman Theater; **Bob GALE,** screenwriter/producer (*Back to the Future*); **Bob GARFIELD,** National Public Radio humorist; **Bob KNOLL,** head of Auto Test Division of *Consumer Reports* magazine; **Bob KOWALSKI,** author, *Eight-Week Cholesterol Cure* ; **Bob MATHIAS,** Olympic decathlon gold medalist; **Bob McALLISTER,** former host of TV's *Wonderama*; **Bob McGUIRE,** host of *Bob McGuire's Outdoor Journal* ; **Bob "Bob 1" MOTHERSBAUGH,** first of two Bobs in rock group Devo; **Bob MOULD,** musician; **Bob PAYTON,** Chicago-style restaurateur in Europe; **TOMATO Bob POLENZ,** tomato farmer/actor; **Bob SCHIEFFER,** CBS News chief Washington correspondent; **Bob SHEA,** historical novelist; **Bob SIROTT,** TV news anchor; **Bob STUPAK,** owner, Bob Stupak's Vegas World Hotel and Casino; **Bob THOMAS,** Hollywood columnist; **Bob WELCH,** musician; **Robert "Bob" Anton WILSON,** science fiction author; **Bob WOLF,** ad agency CEO

PART FOUR: THE BOB APPENDIX

I N T R O D

by Bob Greene

Back in 1985 there was a big storm in the Atlantic Ocean. The storm was so big that it was upgraded to a hurricane.

Specifically, it was upgraded to Hurricane Bob.

This dismayed a lot of us, because we knew what was going to come next. Every TV weatherman and newscaster had a little smirk on his face every time he mentioned Hurricane Bob. The broadcasters couldn't help it; there was something inherently funny about Hurricane Bob. Hurricane Bob, they would say, and the smiles would start to creep onto their faces. Hurricanes are supposed to frighten people; Hurricane Bob made the newscasters giggle.

It was hard to blame the newscasters. Bob is a dumb name. It's a clunky name. Bob is the plain, boring, sensible shoe of names. Bob sounds like a cork dipping up and down in the water.

I have never been able to escape this, of course, and Hurricane Bob only served to remind me. On the computer system at the newspaper where I work, when I log on every morning the screen flashes a message at me: "Welcome to the Editorial System, Bob." I always feel that the screen is laughing.

Thus, I have this nagging feeling that David Rensin and Bill Zehme—the authors of the book you are now holding in your hands—were laughing at me when they asked me to write this introduction. Oh, they weren't laughing when they made the request; they somberly told me what an honor it was for me, out of all the Bobs in the world, to be the one Bob selected to write the introduction to *The Bob Book*. But I know that as soon as I was out of earshot they doubled over with laughter.

Bob. Bob. Bob. Down through history, men of valor and achievement have seldom been named Bob. The great figures in literature are not named Bob. Think about it. There's Bob Cratchit in Dickens's *A Christmas Carol*—and let's face it, Cratchit was not exactly a dashing, dream-inspiring vagabond. After Cratchit the list of literary Bobs grows pretty short.

There has never been a President of the United States named Bob. Thomas, yes. John, yes. Martin and Zachary and Millard and Warren and Ulysses and Rutherford and Chester and Grover and Woodrow—yes. But never a President Bob. In all of our 200-plus years as a nation, the people of America have never taken it upon themselves to make a Bob their president.

I'm not much of a student of British history, but if there was ever a King Bob,

I'm not aware of it. And it's no wonder; the name is not the stuff of legends, which is why we have never heard about the exploits of Bob the Lionhearted.

The main anchormen for the big commercial television networks' evening news programs have never been named Bob, either. Walter and Dan and Tom and John and Peter and David—over the years all of them have read the evening news. Not Bob, though. In television terms, Bob is just the guy who flies up from Washington to substitute on the weekend newscasts.

The most dashing movie stars have not been Bobs either. Gary, Kirk, Errol—of course. Think about a Bob in the movies, and you come up with Bob Cummings. Those talented actors who have been born with the name Robert have taken the wise course and not shortened it—Robert Mitchum is one example. But if a movie star wants to be memorable, he is best advised to stay away from Bob. James Dean would have caused nary a ripple if he had called himself Bob Dean. In the world of popular culture, who would have ever screamed for Bob Presley? The Beatles would never have gotten out of Liverpool had their names been John, Paul, George, and Bob. When you think of Crosbys, Bing is the one who immediately comes to mind. There was a Bob Crosby, but he sort of fades into your brain. That's how it is with Bobs. The world would never have noticed one of its greatest singing talents if the young crooner who came out of New Jersey had been saddled with the name Bob Sinatra.

One way for Bobs to get out of this dilemma is for them to go with Bobby. A lot of teen-idol rock-and-roll stars did that in the early years, with remarkable success. Bobby Vee sold millions of records; Bob Vee sounds like a small-time embezzler. Bobby is a good name for athletes; a Bobby is a scrambling quarterback or an elusive running back. Bob? The team trainer.

But grown men, if they aren't singers or athletes, have trouble going around calling themselves Bobby. Although a lot of us have a secret—our families still call us Bobby, even though the rest of the world calls us Bob. Yes, even our mothers instinctively know that Bob is a dumb name. Even our mothers try to avoid using it.

Our history would be so much duller had the great men of fiction and real-life accomplishment been named Bob. F. Scott Fitzgerald's *The Great Gatsby* is often called the finest novel of all time; had Fitzgerald decided to make Jay Gatsby into Bob Gatsby, no one would have paid any attention to the book. The memory of Franklin Delano Roosevelt still brings tears to many people's eyes; do you think Bob Roosevelt would have attracted a dozen votes? Joe DiMaggio was perhaps the greatest sports figure of his time; how many fans do you think would have lined up to see Joltin' Bob DiMaggio?

Nevertheless, David Rensin and Bill Zehme—born with fine, sturdy, firm-jawed American first names—succeeded in persuading me to write the introduction to *The Bob Book*, saying that the book will be a stirring tribute to Bobs everywhere. They also told me that they know I am accustomed to being paid for my writing, but that doing *The Bob Book* is virtually a labor of love for them—they made it sound as if they are doing it as a public service. Thus, they told me that I should feel proud to be writing this introduction for free; if, on the off chance, *The Bob Book* should become an enormously successful international bestseller, Rensin and Zehme assured me that they "certainly will reconsider" the question of compensating me for my time and effort. I mention this only to point out another lamentable quality about Bobs: We are very gullible.

So that's about it, except for one thing. Remember Hurricane Bob, which we mentioned at the beginning of this little essay?

After only one day, Hurricane Bob was downgraded to a tropical depression. That figures.

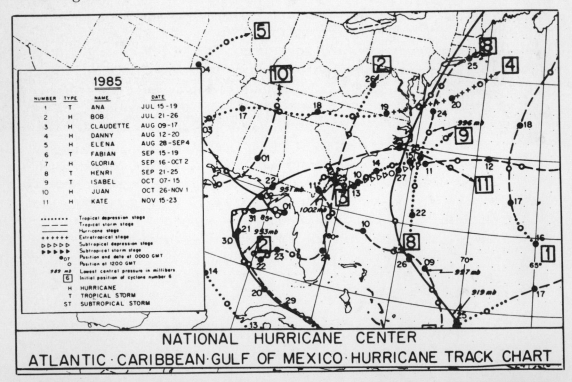

The path of Hurricane Bob, 1985

"**W**hen I started in vaudeville, I found myself starving in Chicago. I was 25. In those days, I was Leslie Townes Hope. I couldn't get a date. Nobody would see my act. I had started in Cleveland, my hometown, where I was getting $10 a show. Then I played Detroit, for $10 a show. In Chicago, though, I couldn't get a date. I was just about ready to go back to Cleveland to get my laundry done and a full meal, when I decided to change my name. I thought, 'Hey, Leslie's a girl's name! I think what I'll do is change it to Bob. It's more chummy; Bob Hope is more chummy than Leslie Hope. There's a little more warmth to it.' Leslie had a little question mark behind it, you know? The next booking agent I went to see looked at me and said, "Would $25 a show be all right?" And I gulped. I said, "Yeah, that'll be fine." I mean, I'd been so hungry, I had just eaten my Adam's apple the night before. So I played three shows as Bob Hope and got hired down the street for $200 a week, then $250 a week! Big money, you know?

"And so I was Bob. *Never stopped* after that.'"

—Bob Hope

PART ONE:

THE MEANING OF BOB

1 WHY BOB?

Bob's BIG BOY RESTAURANTS

"People do a quicker fix on Bobs than on Joes and Jacks." —**BOB VILA**

Bobs are alike.

They have much in common. They have more in common than people who inhabit other names. Johns, for instance, are pretty much a mixed bag. They come in all flavors. Bobs enjoy a solid sense of sameness. Bobs are undiluted. Bobs are universal.

Bobs simplify life.

They are just and plain and just plain.

Most every Bob is a decent, dependable sort.

In a world gone mad, life for Bob is always a manageable task. Bobs tend to know where they are going. They implicitly steer clear of chaos. They are essentially unaffected. In a society choked with pretentiousness, Bobs have little to prove. If they wanted to prove anything, they would call themselves Robert. Or Rob. Or Bobby. Or Sting.

Bob is more than a name; Bob is more than a verb. Bob is the actor who played Gilligan. Bob is the first double-decker hamburger. Bob is Bing Crosby's less famous brother. Bob is Captain

Kangaroo. Bob pulled Howdy Doody's strings. Bob entertains the boys overseas at Christmas. Bob works overtime for Ebenezer Scrooge.

Bob is always there.

Bob does what he is supposed to do and he does it without fanfare. Bobs are never overwhelmed by circumstances; they face the music one note at a time. They do not dance; they hum. There is nothing flashy about Bobs. They put forth only what they are capable of expending; they can afford to promise little more. It's not as though they can hide behind their name. There isn't room.

There is a lesson to be learned from Bobs.

It is a lesson in realism, honesty, and simple pleasure.

It is a lesson no Bob can teach.

Bobs would never be that presumptuous.

> *"Bob is a good boy's name. Better than Clarence, Oscar, or Elmer."*
> —BUFFALO BOB SMITH

WHAT NO BOB KNOWS

Here is the tricky part: Being a Bob means not quite knowing what being a Bob means.

15

BOB LURIE GLASS CORP
24 Hour Answering Service
6960 N Teutonia Av ———————— 351-0400
Bob & Mary's Upholstery Shop ——— 242-3880
Bob Nolan For Lt Governor
921-A Madison Av ———————— 762-7700
Bob Obst Insurance Agcy
13620 Capitol Dr ———————— 781-4409
Bob On North barbr 6439 W North Av —— 475-6667
Bob Paul's Auto & Tire Center
9435 W Lincoln Av ———————— 327-2227
Bob Quirk Insurance Agcy
910 Elm Grove Rd ———————— 784-4666
Bob Rinderle Tire Co 2079 S 35 ——— 384-7830
Bob Sommerfeld Asphalt Inc ——— 542-0770
Bob Sparks Photography
6633 W Mt Vernon Av ———————— 258-6840
Bob Tallinger Appraisal Services
S31 W24661 Sunset Dr Wksh ——— 544-4066

BOB TOLKAN BUICK—
2 Minutes South Of 894
5700 S 27 ———————— 282-3000
Parts Dept 5700 S 27 ———————— 282-3010
Bob Tuttle's Arco 1505 E Capitol Dr ——— 964-3030
BOB TUTTLE'S TIRE & AUTO
SERVICE CENTER INC—
1505 E Capitol Dr ———————— 964-0505
1505 E Capitol Dr ———————— 964-3030
Bob Winter Builders
W220 N8258 Townline Rd Men Fls —— 251-2242
Bob Zoulek's Mid City Plumbing &
Heating Inc 12930 W Custer Av Butler —— 781-5940
BOBKE PAINT INC—
11928 W Greenfield Av ———————— 453-4012
4413 W Lisbon Av ———————— 442-3323
Bob's Auto Clinic 6000 W Natl Av —— 453-9915

BOB'S AUTOMOTIVE
SERVICE INC
7 AM-6 PM Sat 8 AM-1 PM
6000 W Villard Av ———————— 463-4443

Bob's Bait Shop Inc 1126 S 108 ——— 453-2460
Bob's Barber Shop 9209 W Blu Mnd Rd — 774-4848
Bob's Barber Shop
6111 W Mequon Rd 112N Mequon——— 242-4020
Bob's Business Inc 4475 N 124 ——— 783-5666
Bob's Cafe 3710 W Vliet ———————— 931-8676
Bob's Capitol Plaza Barber Stylist
15640 Capitol Dr ———————— 781-7970
Bob's Coins 8307 W Becher ——— 541-8650
Bob's Color Corner
N88 W16650 Appleton Av Men Fls —— 251-4411
Bob's Electric Service
N26 W22219 Glenwood La Wksh —— 544-4661
Bob's Flower Shop 9209 W Center —— 774-6767
Bob's Fruits 16880 W Natl Av New Brln — 784-3658
BOB'S GLASS SERVICE
1701 S 68 ———————— 475-0748

BOB'S GLASS SERVICE
INC 637 W St Paul Av Wksh ——— 547-3060

Bob's Kwik-Print 7817 W Brown Deer Rd —— 354-6811
BOB'S MAYTAG CENTRAL
SERVICE CO 1400 N 118 ——— 781-7080
Bob's Micro Service ———————— 527-4214
Bob's Movin' Inn 1900 S Muskego Av —— 383-4186
Bob's OK Coin Store 3159 S 13 ——— 643-5775
Bob's Oval Bar 9141 W Natl Av ——— 545-8818
Pizza & Italian Cooking

No Bob fully understands what the big deal is. The big deal is that there is no big deal. Bob thinks that he is nothing special and, in fact, he isn't—which is exactly what makes him so special. Bob downplays. He demurs. He shrugs frequently. While not quite shy, Bobs don't toot their own horns. No Bob, for instance, would dare assemble a book such as this one. No Bob celebrates being Bob; Bobs celebrate raises, births,

> "A Bob has a sense of humor, knows how to watch a ballgame, and is somebody with whom you can sit in silence." —BOB BRAVARD, library director

softball victories, and the onset of Fridays. No Bob in the history of mankind has ever exclaimed, "Hey, my name is Bob! Isn't that fabulous! I'm a Bob! Look at me! I'm Bob!"

Bob is the opposite of fabulous.

Bob rarely exclaims unless a car has backed over his foot.

Bob wants no one to look at him for very long, unless the look is the look of love, and even then a sidelong glance is preferable.

Bob has work to do.

A WORLD WITHOUT BOB

Imagine a world without Bobs. While no Bob demands to be noticed, we would miss Bobs if they weren't around. As with water, we would be most aware of Bobs if there were no more Bobs to take for granted. Without Bobs, society would lack grounding. For Bob is the good earth from which there springs tangle and flora. Bob provides balance. Bob is the cake so that others may be the icing. Which is the way Bobs like it. Along these lines:

• Bobs are basic so that others may be hifalutin.

• Bobs are straightforward so that others may be elliptical.

• Bobs are easy so that others may be difficult.

• Bobs are honorable so that others can screw us over.

Among accessible kinds of guys, Bobs truly define *accessible, kind of,* and *guy.* No Bob is fearsome. No Bob embodies threat. No Bob instills trepidation. The beauty of a Bob is that you can walk right up to him, do what needs to be done, say what needs to be said, and get on with business. You may even get change back and, if you do, don't bother counting it. Bobs give you what you're supposed to get. There are no hidden agendas with Bobs. Bob is the apogee of approachability, the soul of informality, the host of *The Price Is Right.* Bobs have better things to do than make your life a living hell. Bobs would rather assemble patio furniture.

THE FAR SIDE By GARY LARSON

Chronicle Features. 1981 Larson 9-24

"So! . . . Out bob bob bobbing along again!"

JUST SAY BOB

Brevity is the soul of Bob.

Bob is a wink of a word. It wastes no time. It is so economical it's hardly even there, really. Bobs take pride in this. They love that it spells easily and spells the same, backward and forward. Bob is Bob, any way you look at it (and him). Bob begins where he ends and ends where he begins. Bob, then, is a palindrome, much like pip, boob, tot, and wow—only with a bit more dignity.

And yet, with all due respect, Bob is a slightly foolish word. It declines to be taken seriously. It is spare, but hardly austere. It is pleasantly puckish. Bob puts one in the mind of fishing tackle and floating apples and jaunty hairdos and carnival rides. Bob recalls the red, red robin's preferred mode of travel. In the fifties, school-girls sauced their conversations with bob-talk (youbob, mebob, shebob).

Which is to say, Bob is fun to say. Few names, in fact, are as much fun, with the possible exception of Hoyt, but then how many Hoyts do you know? Bob, on the other hand, is everywhere.

Try saying Bob now. Let "Bob" roll off your tongue. That's right: the truth of the matter is that saying "Bob" requires no tongue at all. Which is the point, as well as the essence of Bob, if you will. No muss, no fuss, no tongue.

Gary Larson is reprinted by permission of Chronicle Features, San Francisco, CA.

bob[1] (bob), *n., v.,* **bobbed, bob·bing.** —*n.* **1.** a short, jerky motion: *a bob of the head.* —*v.t.* **2.** to move quickly down and up: *to bob the head.* **3.** to indicate with such a motion: *to bob a greeting.* **4.** to make a jerky motion with the head or body. **5.** to move about with jerky, usually rising and falling motions: *The ball bobbed upon the waves.* **6. bob up,** to emerge or appear, esp. unexpectedly: *A familiar face bobbed up in the crowd.* [1400–50; late ME *bobben.* See BOB[2]]

bob[2] (bob), *n., v.,* **bobbed, bob·bing.** —*n.* **1.** a style of short haircut for women and children. **2.** a docked horse's tail. **3.** a dangling or terminal object, as the weight on a pendulum or a plumb line. **4.** a short, simple line in a verse or song, esp. a short refrain or coda. **5.** *Angling.* **a.** a knot of worms, rags, etc., on a string. **b.** a float for a fishing line. **6.** a bobsled or bob skate. **7.** *Scot.* a bunch, cluster, or wad, esp. a small bouquet of flowers. **8.** *Obs.* See **walking beam.** —*v.t.* **9.** to cut short; dock: *They bobbed their hair to be in style.* —*v.i.* **10.** to try to snatch floating or dangling objects with the teeth: *to bob for apples.* **11.** *Angling.* to fish with a bob. [1300–50; ME *bobbe* (n.) spray, cluster, bunch (of leaves, flowers, fruit, etc.); of uncert. orig.]

bob[3] (bob), *n., v.,* **bobbed, bob·bing.** —*n.* **1.** a tap; light blow. **2.** a polishing wheel of leather, felt, or the like. —*v.t.* **3.** to tap; strike lightly. [1350–1400; ME *bobben* to strike, beat, perh. imit. See BOP[2]]

bob[4] (bob), *n., pl.* **bob.** *Brit. Informal.* a shilling. [1780–90; perh. from BOB]

Bob (bob), *n.* a male given name, form of **Robert.**

Bo·ba·dil·la (bô′vä the′lyä, -the′yä), *n.* **Fran·cis·co** ... -sēs′-), died 1502 ...

BOB UECKER ON BEING BOB

Bob Uecker is Mr. Baseball. More than any Bob, he is famous for his mediocrity. In fact, he has traded on it: in his career, he has been an entirely forgettable major-league catcher, the radio voice of the Milwaukee Brewers, a sitcom actor, and the butt of many Miller Lite commercials. Mostly, however, he is Bob.

"Bob means getting away from patent leather shoes," said Uecker. "Roberts are into that. Also pants with a stripe. Robert has always sounded tuxedo-ish to me. Robert McFarlane. Robert Morley. Bob's one of the guys, you know. For instance: 'Bob on up and kiss my ass.' You couldn't say, 'Robert up and kiss my ass. It's got to be Bob.'" —from *Playboy's* 20 Questions Copyright 1987 by *Playboy.*

MOST POPULAR NAMES: ROBERT	
England	USA
1700 - 6th	1875 - 8th
1800 - 9th	1900 - 4th
1850 - 9th	1925 - 1st
1875 - 16th	
1900 - 11th	1940 - 1st
1925 - 6th	1950 - 1st
1950 - 6th	1960 - 3rd
1965 - 9th	
1975 - 13th	1970 - 2nd
1985 - 13th	1984 - 17th

A Bob by Any Other Name...

From Robert there springs Bob and Bob springs eternal. Bob does not show up on most birth certificates. The name is rarely given to newborns.

In 1988, only nine boys in California were born Bob. Compared to 3,641 Roberts, the eighth most popular name. In 1983, Robert was the 13th most popular name, nationally.

In the 1950s only three in 10,000 American babies were born Bob. That same year in Canada, the ratio was one in 10,000.

Here are some more facts about Robert. Draw your own conclusions about Bob.

2   WHO IS BOB?

"All guys think I look like somebody who was in the service with them and all women think I look like their first husband." —BOB NEWHART

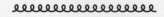

Bob is any one of the seven guys who look up when someone calls out "Bob!" in a crowded space.

Bobs are good that way.

Bobs are easy to spot because when one enters a room, people will say, "Hi, Bob." Bob Newhart is one such Bob, although there are countless others. What's special about Newhart is that he had a television series on which people said hello to him every several seconds. He is the Bob who has been greeted more than any other for the sake of popular entertainment. College students dedicate drinking contests to this phenomenon; they study his reruns and chug alcohol whenever Bob is greeted. This is called the "Hi, Bob" game. Such is Bob's cultural influence.

But Bobs are much more than men who greet well.

Bobs are the fellows who do what's necessary. They work. They eat. They mate. They procreate. They rest. They die. Of course, other men do these things, too—only not with the same sense of purpose. Bobs have greater clarity in such matters. They can't help it. They just do.

To put it another way, Joes are regular. Sams are good. Scotts are great. Bills are paid. Johns are occupied. Dicks are, well…Bobs can be all of the above, but mainly Bobs are just Bobs. Which is all they need to be.

BOB AND FAME

Most Bobs are not famous.

Ironically, Bob—or Robert, at least—is

> *"Bob is a funny word that I hope conveys that I don't take myself all that seriously."* —**BOB MACKIE**

supposed to mean "bright fame." This, of course, is ridiculous. Bobs blanch at lime-light; they squint and shuffle uneasily in the glare. Fame requires a great deal of smiling; Bobs smile only when they are pleased, and nothing pleases Bobs less than the idea of giving press conferences, posing for photographs, and riding pa-rade floats. Bobs smile at sunsets, comely women, and cars with fresh wax jobs. Bobs don't bask in their own achievements; they bask in the achievements of those who play professional sports. Bobs don't sign auto-graphs; they write their name.

When a Bob manages to become fa-mous, it is usually for good reason. Bobs are famous in spite of themselves. Bobs are famous only when they can be nothing else. Fame embraces Bobs; Bobs do not embrace fame. Bobs will, of course, seek out success; they want to do okay for them-selves, to be sure. But fame, should it de-scend upon Bob, is merely complementary. It is like the free coffee

mug you get with a special donut purchase: you earned it, but you're not entirely sure why. Ultimately, Bobs would rather not think about it.

Consider Bob Hope.

Not only is he preeminent among Bobs, Bob Hope is more famous than most Homo sapiens, in general. Bob Hope was born Leslie Hope. Leslie Townes Hope. Leslies, by and large, have fewer problems accepting fame than Bobs do. But who really wants to be famous with a name like Leslie? Plus, Bob fits Hope like snug golf shoes. Bob Hope, once he became Bob Hope, also became the definitive Bob: He isn't flashy. He works tirelessly. He is calm and confident. He doesn't do a lot of emoting. He stays married (perhaps by not being home a lot). He is rigorously patriotic. He is rather frugal. He is there when you need him. He ages gracefully. He's never slept with Madonna.

If any sort of fame truly suits Bobs, it is

sports fame. Bobs can enjoy sports fame in a way they can't with other versions of fame, mainly because athletes generally operate under the delusion that no one except their opponents watch them work. Athletes are trained to pretend that all

> *"Being Bob means that almost everyone treats you as if they'd known you for years—even if it's the first time they meet you."*
> —BOB CUMMINGS

those people in the stands don't really exist, that crowd noise is probably just low-flying air traffic. This is very liberating for Bobs.

American sport is densely packed with Bobs, which is as it should be: Bobs come to play. Bobs keep their eye on the ball.

Doonesbury

BY GARRY TRUDEAU

Dr. Whoopee peddles contraceptives to a discreet faux Bob.

SPORTS BOBS

BASEBALL: Bob Bailey; Bob Boone; Bob Feller; Bob Forsch; Bob Gibson; Bob Horner; Bob Lemon; Bob Lillis; Bob Skinner; Bob Tewksbury; Bob Turley; Bob Walk; Bob Watson; Bob Welch; GOLF: Bob Cupp; Bob Gilder; Bob Lohr; Bob Mann; Bob Rosburg; Bob Toski; Bob Tway; FOOTBALL: Bob Bruzinski; Bob Griese; Bob Hayes; Bob Lilly; Bob Waterfield; BASKETBALL: Bob Cousy; Bob Lanier; Bob Love; Bob McAdoo; Bob Petit; OLYMPICS: Bob Beamon; Bob Ctvrtlick; Bob Mathias; Bob Richards; Bob Seagren; RACING: Bob Bondurant; WRESTLING: Bob Luce; Bob Orton. HOCKEY: Bob Gainey, Bob Probert; BOWLING: Bob Chase, Bob Kwolek, Bob Strampe.

Bobs give 110 percent. Plus, they look damned good in uniform (uniforms celebrate sameness in a way Bobs inherently must admire). Moreover, Bobs excel in the sports interview process. Since there is never anything very interesting to ask an athlete—"You looked great out there today! What are your thoughts on that?"— Bobs are safe from having to delve into areas of deep personal introspection. A few quick clichés, a simple "110 percent" acknowledgment, and it's straight to the showers. What Bob couldn't handle that?

24

A BOB IN LIGHTS

Bob Newhart recalls the singular irony of seeing his name in lights:

"Bob is the kind of name that looks silly in lights. There was a time in Las Vegas when performers didn't even bother with last names on marquees. It was just 'Sammy' and 'Frank' and 'Wayne' and 'Elvis.' Even Rich Little was 'Rich.' They all had Vegas closings, where, in the midst of a laser show, a sign came down with their name on it. And my wife Ginny said to me, 'Gee, it would be funny if you came out and did a Bob number.' So we worked up this elaborate dance number, a spoof Fred Astaire–Gene Kelly adagio, with a socko closing. We did it at the MGM Grand: a closing act to end all closing acts. I wore a top hat and tails and, as the orchestra played 'Stairway to Paradise,' I climbed an actual staircase on which the steps would light up, one at a time, as I ascended them, while singing in a bad falsetto. At the top tier, a pair of heavyset twin chorines tore off my tuxedo and chased me. Cannons went off, spewing confetti. And finally an enormous BOB sign came down. I climbed into the 'O,' sat down, and rode it up into the rafters. The look on the faces of the people in the audience was worth the whole thing. They simply stared in disbelief at what had just transpired."

—Bob Newhart

BOB'S OCEAN

BOBLAND

CAPE BOB

PORT BOB

BOB'S VINE-YARD

BOB HARBOR
BOBHAMPTON

SOUTH BOBVILLE

BOBVILLE

NORTH BOBVILLE

LONG BOB ISLAND

BOB NARROWS

TO THE LESSER BOBBLES

KEY BOB-O

BOB'S POND

GULF of BOB

BOB'S CREEK

BOB'S INLET

BOB'S BEACH

BOB'S BIRTHPLACE
(FORMERLY "RALPHVILLE")

BOB'S PEAK

MT. BOB

THE GREAT BOB MOUNTAINS

BOBAPOLIS

BOB STATE
(HOME OF THE
BOBCATS)

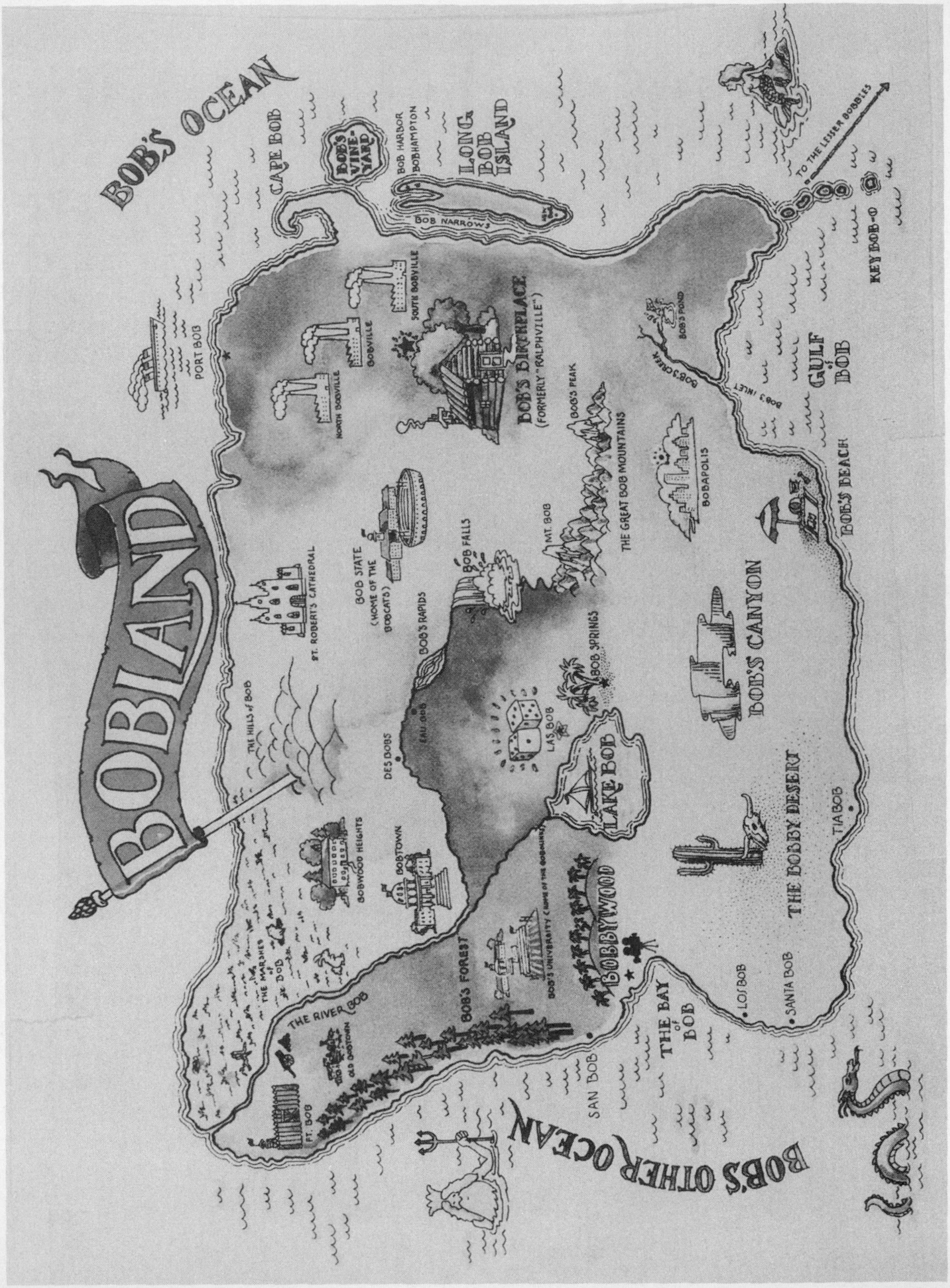

PT. ROBERT'S CATHEDRAL

BOB FALLS

BOB'S RAPIDS

BOB'S CANYON

BOB SPRINGS

THE HILLS of BOB

DES BOBS

BOB'S LAKE

LAS BOB

LAKE BOB

BOB'S BEACH

THE BOBBY DESERT

TIA BOB

BOBWOOD HEIGHTS

BOBTOWN

BOBBYWOOD

BOB'S UNIVERSITY (HOME OF THE BOBORINES)

SANTA BOB

LOL BOB

THE MARSHES of BOB

THE RIVER BOB

BOB'S FOREST

OLD BOBTOWN

THE BAY of BOB

SAN BOB

FT. BOB

BOB'S OTHER OCEAN

BOB IN AMERICA

Bob is America.

It isn't as though Bobs don't thrive in other lands. Hope, after all, was born in England. Then there is **Bob** Hawke, Prime Minister of Australia. Film actor **Bob** Hoskins is British. Musician **Bob** Geldof is Irish, although he was later knighted by the Queen of England, thereby making him Sir **Bob**. We know of a **Bob** Shop in Paris, **Bob**'s Youth Hostel in Amsterdam and a **Bob** Restaurant around the corner from the Taj Mahal. Wherever civilization needs a foothold in unflinching reality, there will be a Bob.

No Bob, however, has ever been elected President of the United States. Few Bobs possess the temerity to try. Bobs do hold many elected offices in the political arena, but shooting for the Big One requires more brio than most Bobs feel comfortable summoning. **Bob** Dole, the Republican senator from Kansas, made some noble attempts, but allowed himself to be called Robert throughout much of his presidential campaigning. Roberts don't instill the same sense of trustworthiness. (No Roberts have been President, either.)

Still, Bobs canvas almost every aspect of American life. Well-known examples abound. Here are but a few: **Bob**s, for instance, edit periodicals as diverse as *The Wall Street Journal* (**Bob** Bartley), the *New Yorker* (**Bob** Gottlieb), *Penthouse* (**Bob** Guccione), and *Soldier of Fortune* (**Bob** Brown). There is Texas-based mock reli-

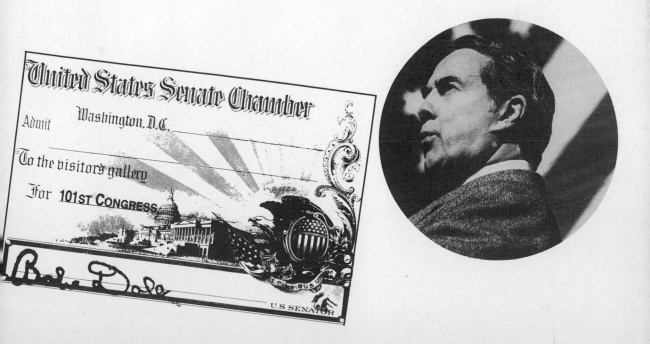

gion whose deity is called **Bob** (technically, J.R. "**Bob**" Dobbs). Morris the Cat and Lassie are owned by **Bob**s (**Bob** Martwick and **Bob** Weatherwax, respectively). **Bob**'s Big Boy, founded by

> *"Being Bob means you can't hide much behind three letters, especially when you can see right through one of them."* —BOB BOLYARD, secretary

Bob Wian, served up the double-decker hamburgers that McDonald's would later seem to emulate with the Big Mac. There was a Postmaster General **Bob** (Preston R. "**Bob**" Tisch). There was the Gay **Bob** doll, a 1970s' cult novelty item; like so, the mysterious "**BOB**" of TV's *Twin Peaks* is much the same for the early nineties. History was altered, in part, by the efforts of one **Bob** Woodward of *The Washington Post*, the reporter who helped

bring down President Richard M. Nixon. **Bob** Redford played **Bob** Woodward in the movie version. **Bob** Culp, in this regard, was **Bob** in *Bob & Carol & Ted & Alice*, the movie that later became a television series featuring **Bob** Urich as **Bob**. **Bob** Cummings once starred in a sitcom called *Love That **Bob***, providing the language with a phrase no **Bob** tires of hearing. It took a **Bob** to throw the book at defrocked televangelist Jim Bakker; Justice Robert "Maximum **Bob**" Potter gave Bakker maximum sentencing for fraud. (**Bob**s hate frauds and evangelists and think there is little difference.) Montana's vast **Bob** Marshall Wilder-

Bob Marshall at the Bob Marshall Wilderness

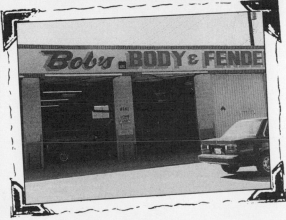

Bob is everywhere: A cornucopia of Bob's businesses including The Bob Shop in Paris, upper right; and the Bob Restaurant, lower right, near the Taj Mahal

ness—known to outdoors enthusiasts simply as The **Bob**—is so named for the **Bob** who thought to preserve the land. Luck would have it that **Bob** Castleberry, a salesman from Denton, Texas, was the $10-million winner in the 1989 Publishers Clearing House sweepstakes, and soon after became the mayor of his hamlet. Luck figures, as well, on Wall Street, where an enterprising **Bob**, **Bob** Golub, sells **Bob**'s Lucky Pota-

toes to superstitious traders. Tomato **Bob** (or **Bob** Polenz) grows legendary red produce in Ringoes, New Jersey, with which he supplies New York's finest restaurants. **Bob** Vlasic devoted his life to the pickle (Vlasic Pickles), as has **Bob** Evans to the pork sausage (**Bob** Evans Farms of Columbus, Ohio and twelve other states). **Bob**: The connective tissue of contemporary society? Or just a guy who gets around?

=LEGEND OF NOBOB=
Nobob was named for a man named Bob, who disappeared from a survey party. Those who searched, upon meeting each other, would say "NO BOB!"

NO BOB, KENTUCKY, AND THE BOB WHO LIVES THERE

Once there was a town where no Bobs dwelled. This town was called No Bob. Eventually, one Bob would live in No Bob, but that didn't change anything.

No Bob, with a population of 50, nestles in the rolling countryside of western Kentucky, deep in Barren County. The origin of No Bob is a tragic one. A Bob lost his life for the sake of the name. But then again, he may have just been misplaced.

The Bob in question was a member of an early-19th century surveying party. Each day all the men would spread out and go about their work and return in the evening to their camp. One evening, the party was missing a member—Bob. Each night they would meet up and ask, "No Bob?" And each

night the answer was, "No Bob." Legend has it that Bob was either eaten by a lion or he was captured by surly local Indians who did him in.

Local color notwithstanding, our investigation of No Bob unearthed a startling discovery: a Bob. His name is Bob Lawson, and as is a Bob's wont, he pays little heed to the existential irony that is his life. He lives in No Bob and just doesn't care. More remarkable still, attached to his property there stand two beech trees twisted together in the shape of the letter "N," as in No Bob. According to local historians, this is the No Bob Tree. Bob's No Bob Tree. And this is Bob:

THE BOB OF NO BOB SPEAKS

How did you come to live in No Bob—were you born there?
Nah, I wasn't born there. I moved into the vicinity when I was two years old.

Is it strange being a Bob who lives in No Bob? Do you feel any pressure to be something you're not?
Nah, Nah, I reckon not.

Are there any other Bobs that live in No Bob?
Oh, I don't know of any.

Is Bob your given name?
It's Bobby—B-O-B-B-Y—I sign my name Bobby L. Lawson.

But most people call you Bob?
Well, about half of them do.

Two beech trees near your home allegedly form the letter "N"—as in No Bob? What do you make of this?
Yeah, that's right. I think they look like an "N."

Do you have any hobbies or anything you enjoy doing in your spare time?
Well, I'm a young man, I'm 79 years old.

I reckon work is my hobby.

What is your favorite book?
I just don't know. I read newspapers all the time.

Do you have a favorite movie?
Nah, I don't go to the movies.

Do you have a favorite TV series?
A favorite what?

Television series.
Well, I listen at the news every night.

Do you have a favorite magazine?
Well, *U.S. News and World Report.*

Do you have a favorite breakfast cereal?
A favorite what?

A breakfast cereal, like oatmeal or cornflakes.
Nah, don't go for them much.

Who's your favorite news anchor, like Tom Brokaw or Peter Jennings?
Ha-ha, I don't know.

Do you have a life philosophy?
No.

31

3 WHO ISN'T BB?

"Only the IRS calls me Robert."

—BOB EUBANKS

ꙭꙭꙭꙭꙭꙭꙭꙭꙭꙭꙭꙭꙭ

Bob is not Robert, Bobby, Rob, Robb, or Robby.

Bob is a choice made by men with options. It is a choice that speaks volumes, albeit in an understated sort of way.

Very few Bobs are born Bob. Bobs almost universally start out as Robert, and as formalities tend to dictate, they will sign checks and grim documents as such until they die. They can't fight this; it's just the way things are. Robert means business. For a Bob, however, hiding behind Robert is uncomfortable and not unlike wearing thick wool trousers in the Tropic of Cancer. Robert itches; Bob scratches. Roberts thrive on respect and appearance; they are solemn fellows who will keep their ties knotted at ballgames after work; Roberts loosen up poorly, look incongruous in leisure wear and barbecue aprons, and are rarely playful; they can be persnickety and occasionally impossible.

Bob is not only possible, he is highly probable.

(One fairly common hybrid is Robert "Bob." Career demands force Robert "Bob" on many frustrated Bobs: Robert "Bob"

THE PLANET BOB AND ITS MOONS
ROBERT, BOBBY, AND ROBERTO

Mitchum, Robert "Bob" Goulet, Robert "Bob" Benchley. Robert "Bobs" are for the most part easygoing guys trapped in stuffy professions. This is especially endemic among actors, politicians, industrialists, and funeral directors. To the public they are Robert; to colleagues and friends with whom they can be themselves, they are Bob.)

Almost certainly, every Bob is a former Bobby. This, you can safely wager, is the work of Bob's mother. Bobby is coddled. By puberty, true Bobs grow impatient with Bobby. Bobby is too frothy, too glib. Indeed, those who remain Bobbys throughout adulthood tend to essay bubbliness, a quality inconceivable to Bobs. (Possible exception to the rule: Bobbys from the South.) Bobbys sing and dance, they weep in public, they mince and prance, they occasionally throw metal folding chairs onto basketball courts. Bobbys are overt. Bobs shun overt behavior as a matter of course. Although no Bob is above harboring a secret desire to chase Bobbys around with cattle prods.

Robs bear watching. They are smooth. They can be trouble. (Robbs are worse. The affectation of that extra "b" prompts Bobs to shake their heads and mutter to themselves—this being Bob's preferred method of displaying disapproval. And, come to think of it, approval.)

Robs make prospective fathers-in-law nervous in ways Bobs never do. Robs are often slicksters, operators, lawyers, and sullen Brat Pack movie actors. Bobs, on the other hand, understand wallpaper.

Robbys have no excuse, really. They are just deplorable weenies.

Bobby Burgess
Prancing Mouseketeer

Rob Petrie
Dancing Comedy Writer

Robert Guillaume
Singing Sitcom Curiosity

Rob Lowe
Priapic Pretty Boy

OF NOT BOBS

Robert Morley
Overstuffed Gourmand

Bobby Sherman
Bubblegum Minstrel

Bobby Knight
Chair-tossing Hothead

Robby Benson
Deplorable Weenie

WHY THEY'RE NOT BOB

NAME	CLAIM TO FAME	WHY HE'S NOT A BOB	NAME	CLAIM TO FAME	WHY HE'S NOT A BOB
BABA RAM DASS	Drug-altered Guru	Misleading pronunciation (Bob Aramdass); real first name is Richard; no Bob gurus; personal friend of Timothy Leary.	J. ROBERT OPPENHEIMER	Atom Bomb Creator	Friends called him Oppie (Ahpee); had a flagrant affair with a Communist spy. Read Sanskrit for fun.
ROBERT CONRAD	Pugnacious Battery Pitchman	Go ahead. Call him Bob. We dare you.	ROBERT REDFORD	Aryan Screen God	He's Bob only to those who THINK they're his friend; played anti-Bob Jay Gatsby in film; also played Bob Woodward (see below) in All The President's Men.
ROBERT DE NIRO	Intense Human Chameleon	Too occluded; spookily loses himself in characters; friends call him Bob, Bobby, and Robert, canceling out each as options.	ROBERT REED	Permed Brady Dad	The hair. Look at the hair. What's the deal with the hair?
ROBERT DUVALL	Method Character Actor	Tango enthusiast; his friends call him Bobby. Made a movie with Tom Cruise.	ROBERT SCHULLER	Prolix TV Pastor	Built Crystal Cathedral when brick would have been just fine; talks about religion in pub-
BOBCAT GOLDTHWAIT	Sniveling Comic Presence	Bobcats aren't Bobs. Bobsleds aren't Bobs. Bobolinks aren't			

lic; has perfect hair.

Bobs. Bobs don't wail and whimper in public.

ROBERT HALL
Common Man's Clothier
Was he a store? Was he a man? This much is known for certain. He was all over Bobs like a cheap suit.

ROBERT KLEIN
Well-dressed Comedian
He sang on Broadway. He sings in his act. He's brilliantly neurotic; an example to all Roberts. They need him more than Bobs.

ROBERT LUDLUM
Pretentious Spy Book Author
Uses a cigarette holder. Wears safari jackets. Spends too much free time thinking about Russian intrigue.

ROBERT McFARLANE
Troubled Ex–National Security Adviser
Lied under oath; couldn't get job done, i.e., attempted suicide using Valium.

ROBERT WAGNER
Rerun Heartthrob
A former Bob, known to friends, as R.J.; overly smooth and continental.

ROBB WELLER
Perky Infotainment Host
Once co-hosted *Entertainment Tonight*. Was he born Robbert? Could he have been a Bob?

BOB WOODWARD
Humorless Journalist
Wrote party-poop epic, *Wired*; wouldn't fill out Bob Survey; should deeply consider reverting to Robert. [Redeeming factor: got famous but kept his newspaper job.]

ROBERT YOUNG
All-knowing TV Icon
Insisted on always knowing best; let James Brolin practice medicine; on the other hand, he's a devotee of Sanka and really looks like a Bob.

4 B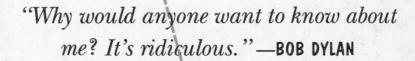BNESS

"Why would anyone want to know about me? It's ridiculous." —**BOB DYLAN**

Slice open any Bob and you will find Bobness.

Bobness is what makes Bobs Bobs.

Bobness is the incorruptible sensibility at Bob's core that defines and regulates his every impulse. Bobness lurks behind every Bob pursuit: Why, for instance, has ineffable game-show host Bob Barker stopped dying his hair brown? Bobness. Why does celebrity handyman Bob Vila love the smell of wet wood, right after a rain? Bobness. Why did Bob Woodward write a book that delivered a knuckle-rub to the memory of dead sybarite John Belushi? Who can say for sure? But it's certain that Bobs do not suffer weakness or excesses gladly. Bobs aren't prudes, but they do hate waste.

If Bobness could be broken down into equal parts, the recipe might be as follows:

- one part pragmatism
- one part dependability
- one part aggressive unpretentiousness
- one part goodheartedness
- one part fear of overt behavior

made fun of. [114] • It's almost impossible to misspell. [198] • My first grade teacher asked everyone ➳

Bobness is the gravity boot that presses Bob's feet firmly to the ground. Bobness is what prevents Bob from wearing berets; from smoking French cigarettes; from quoting Nietzsche, Flaubert, or Gertrude Stein. It accounts for Bobs breaking out in cold sweats whenever in the vicinity of mimes, Renaissance fairs, Vandyke beards, tarot cards, New Age music, and people who say, "*Ciao* !" None of which is to say that Bobness is exclusive to Bobs. Jane Pauley, for instance, is bursting with Bobness. Phil Collins is awash in it. Donald Trump, on the other hand, is entirely devoid of Bobness. And Shirley MacLaine, in this life or any other, has never been nor will she ever be a Bob.

HOW BOBNESS WORKS

It just does.

Bobness doesn't go away. Like quickly digested pastrami, it just sits there and manifests itself. Bobness keeps Bobs honest. For instance, when Bobs become rich, Bobness prevents them from getting showy and aloof. In this regard, the wealthier the Bob, the less wealthy he seems: Bob Hope loves his grilled cheese sandwiches and unsightly golf slacks. Bob Castleberry, the $10-million Publishers Clearing House winner, still walks to the grocer to buy the canned fruit he so enjoys. A great day for Chicago-based billionaire Bob Pritzker is

> *"Bob means that I always got top billing over Ray, though he was much the funnier one."*—**BOB ELLIOT**

CLOSET BOBS

JANE PAULEY

RON HOWARD

GEORGE HARRISON

JOE GARAGIOLA

PAUL HOGAN

ARNOLD PALMER

PAT SAJAK

PRINCE CHARLES

BARBARA BUSH

JOHN McPHEE

PHIL COLLINS

LARRY HOLMES

FRED DRYER

BOB WOODWARD

BARNEY RUBBLE

HARRY ANGSTROM

JIMMY STEWART

MARGE SIMPSON

WHY I'M
BOB

what they wanted to be called. In a moment of youthful exuberance I blurted, "Bob!" [134]

Bob's earthly possessions,
as scribbled on Roseanne Barr's notepad in the
film "She-Devil"

to tour factories and see how stuff works. Bob Tisch, whose Loews Corporation is an $8-billion-ish enterprise, has been known to park cars and haul luggage during labor strikes at his hotels. According to *Manhattan Inc.* magazine, everyone who knows Bob Tisch has a Bob Tisch story that goes like so: "I was with Bob in New York/on the Riviera/in California and we walked into a hotel/restaurant/factory and he not only greeted a bellman/chef/foreman by his first name, he asked about the person's child/parent/spouse." When he

became the nation's postmaster general, one of his mail-world minions remarked after meeting him, "Another postmaster would say, 'Hello, I'm General Tisch.' He just walked up and said, 'Hi, I'm Bob.'"

"I figure Bob is just trying to do the best he can, and make it until Wednesday," said actor Ed Begley, Jr., of the Bob he played in the movie *She-Devil.* His point, of course, is a universal one. It applies to every Bob, like Bob Kerrey, who, in listing reasons why he planned to give up the Nebraska governorship, said he just wanted to clean his own bathroom. Or Bob Ream, a Montana wildlife researcher who imitates wolf howls. His personal Bobness was described in the *New Yorker* in this way: "[Bob] is a large, calm person with an unhurried stride, a Huck Finn grin, and a habit of saying nothing until he has something to say." That Bob is not dissimilar to Florida senator Bob Graham, who makes it his habit to jot in tiny notebooks at every free moment. Lest this seem a frivolous exercise, he will stress, "I don't try to write down what I'm thinking or feeling. It's not

BOB'S BIGGEST FEARS

women

weapons

dancing

bob

the thought of fatherhood

40

a diary. It's pretty pragmatic."

Pragmatism is, as we have said, the cornerstone of Bobness, as well as attorney Bob Nordyke's Salem, Oregon, Drive-up Divorce service. "In Oregon, we have a lot

> "To the kids and their parents who watch Sesame Street, I'm just plain Bob, except for a number of two-year-olds who call me 'Bop.'"
>
> —BOB McGRATH

of rain," Bob explained. "Some people don't want to get out of their cars." Bob Bishop, director of New York's Museum of American Folk Art, is so pragmatic that he wants to split his museum into little museums to be located in shopping malls. Says Bob of his more snooty peers: "They don't want to have anything to do with malls. Museum types are like that: they think malls are beneath them. They don't like it now, but they will." This attitude jibes with the single most profound barometer of Bobness: Bobs not only like the way a La-Z-Boy recliner feels, they actually like the way it looks.

UNFLAPPABLY YOURS
BOBS AT THE MIKE

Ultimate Bobness: Bobs keep their eye on the ball. They aren't easily distracted. As evidence, here's the way Bob "Mr. Baseball" Uecker, radio voice of the Milwaukee Brewers, imagines how Bob Elson, the late, unflappable voice of the Chicago White Sox, would have reacted to an unexpected interruption of his play-by-play broadcast:

" 'It's a swing and a miss, the White Sox haven't won in 21 days, bases loaded here and nobody out. And the Yankees leading two-to-one." Meanwhile, the engineer keeps trying to get his attention. "Wow, our engineer keeps telling me that we have a public service-announcement, but more important, the White Sox have a chance to win this game.

" 'All right, we'll read this thing. Here's a swing and a foul off the bat of Gene Freeze and it's nothing—one. It seems the Russians have launched an ICBM missile attack—here's a ball, low and outside—against the Chicagoland area, and the attack is due to hit here around—here's a swing and a line

drive foul to left—at about 4:30, that is Central Time—but right now, the White Sox with a chance to win this game. Here is the windup and the next pitch. Strike three called, and this game is over. And the White Sox leave the bases loaded. And as we look out over the right-field area here in Comiskey Park, we see some of those missiles exploding in the downtown Chicago area. Now, for those of you who are looking for an escape route out of Chicago, I-94 North seems like your best route. You might want to try 45 West. But don't forget the Red Sox are in for a weekend series starting tomorrow. That's Friday, Saturday, and Sunday. And Sunday is going to be Jersey Day here at the ballpark. Everybody entering the park gets a free cow. So come on out Sunday afternoon when the White Sox take on Boston. Boy, look at those bombs exploding. There goes the right-field seats. So long, everybody.' "

—from *Playboy's* 20 Questions Copyright 1987 by *Playboy*.

THE QUOTABLE BOB :

A treasury of Bobs unwittingly dispensing Bobness.

• *I was in the right place at the right time. Of course I steered myself there.* —Bob Hope

• I love going through factories. Everybody has his own hobbies. That's mine.
—Bob Pritzker, billionaire industrialist

• I heard it's supposed to change your life drastically, but I think if you don't want it to, it won't.
—Bob Castleberry, $10-million winner in Publishers Clearing House sweepstakes

• *I created Bruce Wayne to be a normal human being living in our society. I didn't want a second Superman. Every human can relate to being a Batman. I really am Batman. When I was younger, I looked just like Bruce Wayne.*
—Bob Kane, creator of Batman

• *Frankly, I find other people more interesting than I find myself. One has to make choices in life. That was a choice I made. Maybe it has erected a barrier in my life, but by and large, it has worked for me.* —Bob Woodward, reporter

• *Some people love to take their shirts off and show you their scars, but I don't.*
—Bob Rafelson, director

• My mother made me take piano lessons. I am terrible. I play popular music.   —Rep. Bob Carr (D–Michigan)

• *There are four things in my life. Work, the ballet, reading, and my family. I don't do anything else. I don't have lunches, dinners, go to plays or movies. I don't meditate, escalate, deviate, or have affairs. So I have plenty of time.*
—Bob Gottlieb, editor of the *New Yorker*

• *I'm not enough of an extrovert to go on this show. Really, I don't care for crowds.*
—Bob Eubanks, on the *New Newlywed Game*

• Bob means being as common as dirt and one dollar bills.
—Bob Christgau, rock critic

• I've never been out of this country, but I've been to California. Does that count?
—Bob Bergland, former secretary of agriculture

• *Bob means you're approachable and down-to-earth and when you show up backward no one knows.* —Bob Miller, Governor of Nevada

• *In three words I can sum up everything I've learned about life. It goes on.*
—Robert "Bob" Frost, poet

• We Bobs hate to be overly dependent on others. We like to manage our own fate. —Bob Keeshan, Captain Kangaroo

• *I always hate to remove material that somebody has spent good money on.*
—Bob Vila, celebrity handyman

5 BOB IN HISTORY

> *"Maybe the biggest problem with the world is that there's never been a world leader named Bob."*
>
> —BOB GALE, *Back to the Future* screenwriter

In the annals of humankind, Bobs have dwelled quietly. When they have accomplished great things, they mostly kept it to themselves, for this—and yardwork—is what Bobs do most dependably. They accept the mantle of posterity the way other men accept gifts of unsightly neckwear on Father's Day.

Still, Bobs have certainly made important contributions to society. What is most difficult, however, is pinpointing the origins of Bob. Who, for instance, was the first Bob? Did he have his own toolshed? Did he loan out his tools? Did he live before there was bowling? Would he consider that living? Unfortunately, we may never know. And perhaps that is best. But, for now, we can only offer speculation as to Bob's earliest stirrings.

ORIGIN OF BOB, THE NAME

One of life's essential yet largely unsolvable mysteries centers on

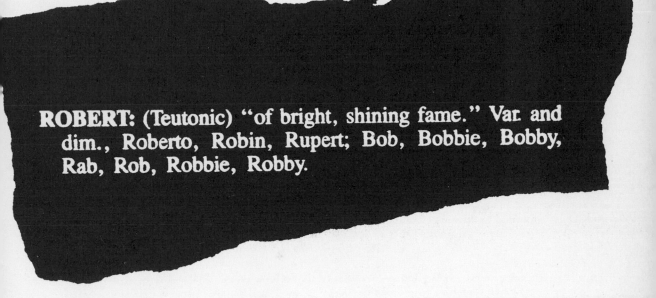

ROBERT: (Teutonic) "of bright, shining fame." Var. and dim., Roberto, Robin, Rupert; Bob, Bobbie, Bobby, Rab, Rob, Robbie, Robby.

when, how, and why Robert became Bob.

Most all Bobs are born Robert. They become Bob by choice; that is, they either choose to be Bob, or choose to accept the name when it is foisted upon them by others.

Bobs are never Bobs by accident.

Historically, Robert is a Norman name, one of many two-element German formations. This one means "fame-bright," and even in Norman times (when it was Hroedebrecht), Robert was one of their half-dozen favorites. The name's popularity continued due to heroes like King Robert the Bruce and General Robert E. Lee. This makes sense since Bob Bruce and Bob Lee would carry little authority on battlefields.

As such, Bob's beginnings are ambiguous. What is known is that Bob was recog-

nized as a "pet form of Robert" around 1721. And although this short form is the most popular today, George Rippey Stewart, author of *American Given Names,* suggests that the shift of an r-sound to a b-sound is unusual. Possible explanations? Perhaps the r-sound was "attracted" by the b-sound already in the name. This is not an uncommon phenomenon lately, at least in the case of the Arby's fast-food restaurant chain.

Other common brief forms of Robert were Hob and Dob, names that would best suit dairy farmers in the Netherlands.

Of course, an l-shift would have been out of the question since Lob, in Middle English, meant a foolish or slovenly fellow. Hardly Bob. Unless, of course, there was a softball game beckoning.

BOB CRATCHIT: THE FIRST GREAT BOB

Charles Dickens created Bob Cratchit in 1843, thus giving the world its first memorable Bob. Cratchit displayed many traits that would inform Bobs for the next century. The evidence, from *A Christmas Carol*:

Bob Makes the Most of a Bad Situation:

"[Bob] put on his white comforter, and tried to warm himself at the candle; in which effort, not being a man of a strong imagination, he failed."

Bob Is Underpaid, But Earns Respect, Anyway:

"Think of that! Bob had but fifteen 'bob' a week himself; he pocketed on Saturdays but fifteen copies of his Christian name; and yet the Ghost of Christmas Present blessed his four-roomed house!"

Bob Projects His Sunny Disposition onto Others:

Asked by his wife how their son behaved during an outing, he responds: "As good as gold…and better."

Bob Takes Simple Pleasure:

"There was never such a goose. Bob said he didn't believe there ever was such a goose cooked."

Bob Flatters His Wife:

"Oh, a wonderful pudding! Bob Cratchit said, and calmly too, that he regarded it as the greatest success achieved by Mrs. Cratchit since their marriage."

Bob Appreciates Productivity:

Upon seeing his wife and daughters sewing: "Bob was very cheerful with them, and spoke pleasantly to all the family. He looked at the work upon the table, and praised the industry and speed of Mrs. Cratchit and the girls."

Bob Feels Guilty When Late for Work:

"The clock struck nine. No Bob. A quarter past. No Bob. He was full eighteen minutes and a half behind his time.…His hat was off, before he opened the door; his comforter too. He was on his stool in a jiffy; driving away with his pen, as if he were trying to overtake nine o'clock."

Bob Is Content in Life:

" 'I am very happy,' said little Bob, 'I am very happy!' "

BOB MARCHES THROUGH TIME

JANUARY

January 1, 1966
The Beach Boys single, "Barbara Ann," which begins **"Bob-Bob - Bob, Bob - Bob - Bobra-Ann"** is released, thereby confusing Bobs for generations to come.

January 2, 1955
The *Love That Bob* television series debuts starring the Bob best known for being loved, **Bob Cummings**; the show runs through September 15, 1959.

January 4, 1943
Bob Hope plays a Bob on film for the first time, in *They Got Me Covered*. He is Robert Kittridge, foreign correspondent.

January 8, 1938
Dimpled game-show host **Bob Eubanks** born in Flint, Michigan.

January 9, 1935
Bob Denver, who will later and forever be Gilligan, although we never know if Gilligan is his first name or last name, is born in New Rochelle, New York.

January 26, 1935
Bob "Mr. Baseball" Uecker is born Robert George in Milwaukee, never dreaming that someday he will become one of the most mediocre catchers in major-league history.

FEBRUARY

February 3, 1945
Miami Dolphin quarterback great **Bob Griese** (Robert Allen) born in Evansville, Indiana.

February 5, 1945
Future reggae king **Bob Marley** (Robert Nesta) born in Kingston, Jamaica.

February 11, 1987
Based on his performance as a prostitute's chauffeur, short, squat Englishbob **Bob Hoskins** nominated for an Oscar for *Mona Lisa.*

February 19, 1934
Bob "Hey, Don't We Have The Same Address?" **Hope** marries Dolores Reade, who will never see much of her peripatetic, workaholic husband, but recognizes him whenever she sees photographs, in Erie, Pennsylvania.

February 21, 1988
Bob Denver reprises his role as beatnik dullard Maynard G. Krebs in the television movie *The Many Lives of Dobie Gillis.*

February 25, 1937
CBS Chief Washington Correspondent **Bob Schieffer**, one of the select society actually born a Bob, is born a Bob in Austin, Texas.

MARCH

March 1, 1974
H. R. "Bob" **Haldeman** denies role after being indicted in Watergate cover-up.

March 4, 1974
H. R. "Bob" **Haldeman** pleads not guilty.

March 7, 1958
Bob Hope plays a Bob on film for the second time, in *Paris Holiday*. He is a thinly disguised version of himself: Robert Leslie Hunter, American Entertainer.

March 17, 1963 — Celtic star **Bob Cousy** is given his own day, Bob Cousy Day, at the Boston Garden.

March 18, 1981 — **Bob Culp** debuts in *Greatest American Hero*. Runs through February 3, 1983.

March 24, 1940 — Future couture to Carol Burnett **Bob Mackie** (Robert Gordon) born in Monterey Park, California.

March 26, 1943 — Watergate sleuth **Bob Woodward** (Robert Upshur) born in Geneva, Illinois.

March 26, 1923 — **Bob Elliot**, who becomes Bob in the quiet, intelligent comedy act, Bob and Ray, is born in Boston, Massachusetts.

March 26, 1990 — Ray Goulding, partner of **Bob Elliot**, and half of the understated comedy team, Bob and Ray, dies at age sixty-eight, leaving Bob Rayless.

March 30, 1910 — Future poobah of pork sausage **Bob Evans** is born down on the farm in Sugar Ridge, Ohio. Will establish national chain for Bob Evans restaurants, celebrated for excellent biscuits in gravy.

APRIL

April 1, 1989 — Celebrity handyman **Bob Vila** leaves the *This Old House* series.

April 3, 1965 — **Bob Dylan**'s "Subterranean Homesick Blues" enters the Top 100 at #94 and peaks at #52. When unintelligible lyrics stymie a nation, Dylan tries to help out by holding up flash cards in the film *Don't Look Back*.

April 7, 1979 — **Bob Seger**'s no-frills rock anthem, "Old-Time Rock & Roll," debuts on charts and later becomes the song that prompts Tom Cruise to dance in his underwear, in the film *Risky Business*.

April 30, 1987 — News is made public that professional emcee **Bob Barker** has donated $250,000 to Primarily Primates, Inc., a wildlife sanctuary in San Antonio, Texas.

MAY

May 1, 1939 — Avenging comic creator **Bob Kane**'s Batman first appears in Detective Comics #27. Kane signs the story "Rob't Kane" but changes it to Bob Kane on the next story and thereafter.

May 6, 1945 — Midwestern rock star **Bob Seger** is born in Ann Arbor, Michigan.

May 6, 1941 — **Bob** "Why Is Everybody Out There Wearing Green?" **Hope** mounts his first performance for American GIs, at March Field, California. From this point on, he will give all of his Christmases to the boys overseas.

May 10, 1988 — Former Nebraska governor and erstwhile Debra Winger boyfriend **Bob Kerrey** wins Nebraska U.S. Senate primary.

May 11, 1981 — Reggae king and dreadlock enthusiast **Bob Marley** dies of cancer in Miami, Florida.

May 15, 1987 — Handbag collector and Elvis fan **Robert "Bob" Gottlieb** takes over as editor of the *New Yorker*.

May 17, 1956 — Future weisenheimer and host of ABC-TV's *America's Funniest Home Videos* **Bob Saget** is born in Philadelphia.

May 24, 1941 — Dependable Enigma **Bob Dylan** is born Robert Allan Zimmerman, in Duluth, Minnesota.

48

May 29, 1903

Bob "You Wouldn't Want To Be Called Leslie, Either" **Hope** is born Leslie Townes Hope in Eltham, England. Four years later he moves to Cleveland and eventually becomes the embodiment of America.

JUNE

June 2, 1965

Bob Hope plays a Bob on film for the third time, in *I'll Take Sweden*. This time he's Bob Holcomb, widower.

June 9, 1910

Love That **Bob Cummings** is born in Joplin, Missouri. Will later remove Ronald Reagan's legs in film *King's Row* and throw a Nazi off of the Statue of Liberty in Hitchcock's *Saboteur*.

June 10, 1935

First day of **Dr. Bob**'s sobriety: Robert Holbrook Smith dries out in Akron, Ohio, and on the same day, not coincidentally cofounds Alcoholics Anonymous.

June 10, 1986

Former Boomtown Rat rocker **Bob Geldof** is knighted Sir Bob by Queen of England, for his efforts to support famine victims by mounting concert extravaganza Live-Aid.

June 12, 1975

Weapon lover **Bob Brown** publishes first issue of *Soldier of Fortune* magazine.

June 17, 1972

Washington Post reporter **Bob Woodward** begins his historic collaboration with Carl Bernstein, covering the arrest of five burglars caught breaking into Democratic Headquarters in the Watergate office-hotel complex.

June 20, 1946

Future celebrity handyman **Bob Vila** born.

June 27, 1927

Stork delivers baby **Bob Keeshan**, who will grow up to wear fanciful bangs and vaguely militaristic clothing, and call himself Captain Kangaroo.

June 29, 1978

Bob Crane, star of *Hogan's Heroes*, is found mysteriously murdered in Scottsdale, Arizona.

JULY

July 4, 1988

Bob Manley leaves Venice, California, with a trailerful of Bobs for *Bob Across America* traveling art tour.

July 13, 1985

Soon-to-be **Sir Bob Geldof** launches Live-Aid.

July 13, 1928

Bob Crane, the man who would be Hogan, is born in Waterbury, Connecticut.

July 22, 1923

Future GOP presidential hopeful **Bob Dole** is born, humbly, in Russell, Kansas.

AUGUST

August 8, 1879

Robert Holbrook Smith—later simply **Dr. Bob**—is born.

August 9, 1928

Short Caucasian **Bob Cousy** (Robert Joseph) born in New York City. Ten-time NBA all-star. Led Boston to five World Championships 1957–63.

August 16, 1930

Robert "Bob" Culp, who would later be Bob in the film *Bob & Carol & Ted & Alice*, is born in Berkeley, California.

August 18, 1937   Future screen WASP **Robert "Bob" Redford** is born Charles Robert Redford, Jr., in Santa Monica, California.

August 22, 1988   Sports mouth **Bob Costas** gets his own interview show that airs in the dead of night on NBC-TV, *Later...with Bob Costas*.

August 22, 1988   **Bob Barker** asks animal lovers around the world to pressure the Hawaii Legislature to ban the use of dogs for pig hunting.

August 24, 1988   Bob, David Letterman's prize German shepherd, dies after a prolonged illness.

SEPTEMBER

September 5, 1929

Gloriously unexciting comic genius **Bob Newhart** is born George Robert Newhart in Chicago, where he will later work as an accountant until he overcomes shyness problem.

September 10, 1948   Basketball's **Bob Lanier** (Robert Jerry, Jr.) born in Buffalo, New York.

September 15, 1965   *I Spy*, starring **Bob Culp** as a fey tennis pro cum secret agent with Bill Cosby as his partner, premieres and runs through September 2, 1968.

September 16, 1972   Hi, Bob: *The Bob Newhart Show*, in which the star portrays stammering Chicago psychologist **Bob Hartley**, premieres. Runs through August 26, 1978. Later, in reruns, the series inspires college students to chug alcohol whenever the phrase "Hi, Bob!" is uttered during episodes.

September 17, 1965   Bob Does the Impossible: *Hogan's Heroes* debuts, starring **Bob Crane** as Colonel Robert Hogan, commanding officer-ringleader of wacky American POWs who conduct sitcom hijinks in Nazi prison camp; viewers don't seem to mind. Runs through July 4, 1971.

September 23, 1987

Director-choreographer-cardiac patient **Bob Fosse** dies twenty-three minutes into the Washington, D.C., premiere of his musical revival *Sweet Charity*. In his will, Bob bequeaths $387.79 apiece to sixty-six of his friends with the Boblike wish: "Go out and have dinner on me."

September 26, 1964   Gilligan and six other castaways wash up on *Gilligan's Island*, which premieres with the great **Bob Denver** in the title role as the chimplike boob who constantly wears a downturned sailor's hat.

September 26, 1973   **Bob Urich** plays Bob Sanders in the short-lived TV version of film *Bob & Carol & Ted & Alice*.

OCTOBER

October 2, 1938   Cleveland Indians ace **Bob Feller** strikes out 18 Detroit Tigers in a nine-inning game, thereby establishing a new major-league record.

October 3, 1955

Mr. Greenjeans' military friend, Captain Kangaroo, makes his TV debut, with **Bob Keeshan** essaying the role of the slightly irritable, but always goodhearted captain. Bunny Rabbit, Mister Moose, and Dancing Bear proudly look on.

October 5, 1954 Future Sir Bob, **Bob Geldof**, born in Dublin, Ireland.

October 16, 1949 Placid Grateful Dead guitarist and second banana **Bob Weir** is born in San Francisco, California.

NOVEMBER

November 9, 1935 Fastball specialist **Bob Gibson**, later known as Hoot during his celebrated career as a St. Louis Cardinal, is born in Omaha, Nebraska.

November 9, 1987 Bob for President: **Bob Dole** announces his candidacy for president with an austerity pledge to achieve a balanced budget.

November 9, 1936 Future governor of Florida, then U.S. Senator **Bob Graham** (Daniel Robert) born in Coral Gables.

November 16, 1950 AA Founder **Dr. Bob** dies—only after happily living out his final days eating great quantities of his favorite dish, meat loaf.

November 26, 1933 Deep-voiced entertainer **Robert "Bob" Goulet** born in Lawrence, Massachusetts.

November 26, 1951 Radio comedy team **Bob and Ray** bring their act to a weekly television format; *Bob and Ray* on TV runs for two years.

November 27, 1917 Howdy Doody's manipulative friend, **Buffalo Bob Smith**, is born, naturally, in Buffalo, New York.

November 28, 1988 **Bob Dole** is reelected by his Republican colleagues to a third term as their Senate leader.

DECEMBER

December 9, 1950 Here Comes the Bob: **Bob Cousy** marries Marie Agnes "Missie" Ritterbusch.

December 12, 1923 Future animal activist and game-show host **Bob Barker** is born in Darrington, Washington, with brown hair, which he will later dye to hide grayness until he realizes what a vain and stupid act this is, and then, doing the Bob thing, embraces the grayness for its honesty and striking realism.

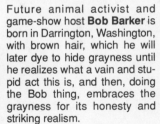

December 17, 1930 Neckchain enthusiast **Bob Guccione** (Robert Charles Edward Sabatini), who will one day publish *Penthouse* magazine, is born in Brooklyn. Guccione, in true Bob utilitarian fashion, will actually photograph his centerfold models himself.

December 19, 1945 **Robert "Bob" Urich**, future star of TV series *Spenser for Hire* and *Vegas*, is born in Toronto, Ontario.

December 24, 1842 Browbeaten clerk **Bob Cratchit** works overtime for difficult employer.

6 THE BOB READER: BOB AS OTHERS SEE HIM

GARRISON KEILLOR'S LAKE WOBEGON BOBS: Bob's Bank

Bob's Bank: Bob's Philosophy

Announcer:...Brought to you by Bob's Bank in Lake Wobegon...

Most banks are large impersonal institutions—you walk in, fill out the forms, shove the paper across the counter, and that's it. It's your money, you do what you like—is the philosophy of the bank.

But that's not Bob's philosophy at Bob's Bank. When you bank with Bob, you are, whether you know it or not, making Bob sort of your dad.

You shove that withdrawal slip across the counter, don't be too surprised if Bob says, "Huh-uh. Not till you tell me what this is for."

Bob used to approve withdrawal slips automatically but no more. Not since he's seen what people withdraw money for—take it out of the bank, throw it around, down one rathole and another—some people you can't trust them with their own money.

Bob got a call the other day from a depositor who was on vacation in Minneapolis and he had gone to a bank to cash a check to get some money for unforeseen vacation expenses, and the bank called Bob to verify the check—Bob said, "Huh-uh. No dice." Couple of small-towners in the big city, dazzled by the bright lights, wanted to withdraw from the principal to pay for fancy meals, another night in an overpriced hotel, some imported goods they coulda got cheaper from Sears. Bob says, "No way."

It's hard at first, but you'll thank him for it someday. It's the bank that looks out for you. Bob's Bank in Lake Wobegon.

—from *A Prairie Home Companion*, from American Public Radio
Copyright © 1987 Garrison Keillor. Reprinted by permission

DINOSAUR BOB

One afternoon, while on safari in Africa, young Scotty Lazardo wandered away from camp. He returned with a dinosaur.

"Look what I caught!" he said.

"Can we keep him?" pleaded Scotty's sisters, Zelda and Velma.

"I don't see why not," said Dr. Lazardo.

"He looks kind of like my uncle Bob," said Mrs. Lazardo.

Jumbu, their bodyguard, said nothing.

Scotty patted the dinosaur on the nose. "Bob?" he tried.

The dinosaur smiled and wagged his giant tail.

So they named him Bob.

—from the children's book
Dinosaur Bob by William Joyce

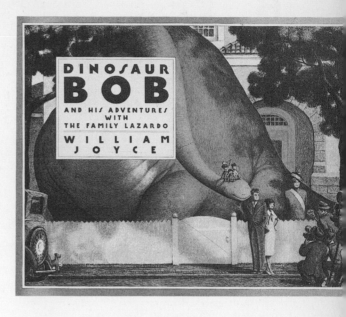

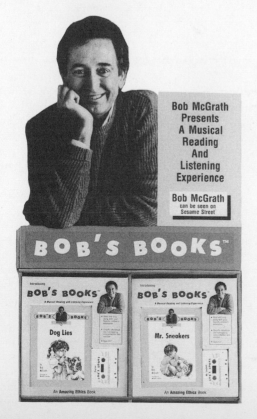

"Had F. Scott Fitzgerald decided to make Jay Gatsby into Bob Gatsby, no one would have paid any attention to the book."

—BOB GREENE

LOUD BOB: A LETTER FROM HELENA, MONTANA

Our friend Bob has disappeared again. He has disappeared often over the years we've known him, and this time, as in the past, we are not alarmed. Bob turns up about once a year, saturates our lives with his presence, then leaves for home. We soon realize that he never told us where home was; or, if he did, we later discover that he isn't living there any longer. Livingston and Missoula, towns east and west of Helena, are reliable guesses. On occasion he telephones from Ironton, Ohio. "Arnton," he pronounces it.

When Bob calls, even long-distance from Ironton, you have to hold the phone far from your ear. Bob yells. Although many myths surround our friend Bob—and this may be one of them—I was once told that his loud voice came from growing up with a partially deaf mother. In his household, everyday conversation was upped a few decibels. "PLEASE PASS THE SALT," you had to say, or, "MOM, THE CAT JUST GOT RUN OVER BY A CAR."

"I'M IN IRONTON," Bob says over the phone when he calls after a long disappearance. "ARNTON."

My husband, Mark, has known Bob since their student days at the University of Montana. According to him, Bob grew up in tent camps and duckblinds in the company of a wildlife-photographer father who dragged the family all over the North American outback to take pictures of bear, moose, elk and other animals. In college, while Mark and Bob fished the Clark Fork one cold spring day, the river swollen with a winter's load of snowmelt, Bob stripped to his underwear, dove in, swam over two hundred yards to the far shore, then swam back again.

Before he vanished the last time, Bob was working as an itinerant hod carrier and attending a weekend massage class in Helena. On Friday nights he would burst into our house, his hair sticking out all over his head. By Saturday, Mark and I would be talking in very loud voices. By Sunday, we were yelling. "IT SURE WAS GREAT TO SEE BOB AGAIN," he screamed at me after Bob left. It took time to turn down the volume again.

Bob is tall and thin and sleeps in his clothes. He favors union suits under jeans, wool lumberjack jackets, and plaid Elmer Fudd hunter hats. I don't know how he makes his fine brown hair stick straight out from his head; it's the classic finger-in-the-socket look.

Not only does Bob yell, his laugh is loud and maniacal, right out of the turn-of-the-century asylums that incarcerated people for ills such as "religious excitement." I love Bob's laugh. How I wish, in the midst of a quarrel with the utilities company or on a flight to Salt Lake City, I could just throw my head back and let one out like Bob does. "FLY DELTA!" I'd yell. Then laugh.

After his last massage class in Helena, just before he drove out of town, and out of contact, Bob took me to lunch at Helena's shelter for the homeless, where he eats occasionally because he likes the people he meets there. I was interested because a rumor in town said the shelter's cook once worked at the Montana Club. It turned out to be the cook's day off, but we ate at the shelter anyway.

After lunch I escorted Bob to his van to say goodbye. Bob's van is a cross between a dumpster and a file cabinet. In the back was a clear plastic sack filled with smashed green herbs the texture of pesto. Winter months in a landscape of snow leave us "white blind"; Bob's plants were so alarmingly green that I gasped and blinked. I thought of the famine in Ireland, when starving people ate grass and walked about with green mouths, dazed; then I imagined Bob, his lips green, laughing his maniac laugh. Should I have packed a dinner for him?

Earlier he had spoken of spending the rest of the winter in Santa Barbara, improving his massage techniques and studying Zen. "YEAH, I'LL GO TO CALIFORNIA," he said with zeal. It's what we all think after the thirty-third consecutive colossal Rocky Mountain snowstorm of the winter.

I said goodbye, and Bob hopped in the van and headed west. About a half hour later, I looked out the window and saw Bob's van roar back down the street. Heading east. We haven't seen him since.

—Ellen Meloy

First appeared in *Wigwag* magazine, March 1990
Reprinted courtesy of *Wigwag* and the authors

PAR FOR BOB TWAY

Standing just off the putting surface, like an uninvited guest, is a six-foot-four-inch earnest-looking young man whose deadpan squint never strays from some private middle distance. This 27-year-old with a perfect helmet of light brown hair and chubby, reddened cheeks—one Bob Tway—is coming off a far better year than any of his illustrious playing partners, but most of those in the gallery that day have no idea who he is.

But striking as Tway's skill is his lack of flamboyance... Tway is a kind of golfing machine almost incapable of playing to the crowd. He doesn't go into a tight macho strut around the green or pump a fist when a putt drops. After a good shot, about all he can muster is a shy smile.

Nor is Tway generous with his emotions off the course. "I'm not ever going to spill my guts," says Tway about his wariness toward the press. Yet Tway's shortcomings as a gallery favorite and news media star are tied to his most attractive qualities. There may never have been a rich young athlete at the top of his sport with a less inflated sense of himself.

—Peter de Jonghe, from "The Golfing Machine,"
in *The New York Times Magazine*

FROM IAN FRAZIER'S "THE END OF BOB'S BOB HOUSE"

In the thirties, it was in the basement of the old Vanderbob Towers Hotel. In the forties, it moved into the first floor of the Youbob Building on Fifty-second Street. In the late fifties, it settled in what was to become its final home, the plush revolving lounge on the top of the BobCo Building. No matter where they found it through the years, patrons of Bob's Bob House (and there were many who were much more than patrons—devotees might be a better word) knew that anyplace old Bob Bobson, God love him, was hanging out, there was sure to be excitement, fun, and big thick steaks nearby. I'll never forget back in '54, I'd just been fired by Bill Veeck for alcoholism, and I walked into the Bob House with a face about a mile long. Bob took one look at me and hollered, "Christ, you're SOBER, Doc!" (He always called me Doc. Of course, I didn't have a medical degree, but I did have my own stapling gun. He called me Doc ever since the war, over in Korea.) "Anything you want, it's on me." My God, I drank the place dry that night, and then I had a good solid piece of grain-fed beef and got in my car and ran over a claims adjuster and ended up in Matteawan State Hospital for the Criminally Insane. That's the kind of guy Bob was.

—Excerpt from *Dating Your Mom*
by Ian Frazier Copyright © 1986 by
Ian Frazier. Reprinted by permission
of Farrar, Straus and Giroux, Inc.

DAVID LYNCH ON BOB'S BIG BOY

Bob's Big Boy, the restaurant chain now owned by the Marriott Corporation, is something of a great American mecca. All manner of Americana—such as the double-decker hamburger—has been born at Bob's. Moreover, David Lynch, director and creator of unique American fare like ABC-TV's *Twin Peaks* and the films *Blue Velvet* and *Wild At Heart*, finds regular inspiration at a Bob's in Los Angeles. *Blue Velvet* was hatched on napkin scribblings at Bob's. The murderer's spirit in *Twin Peaks* was named BOB. Lynch, who slightly resembles Big Boy himself, explains his fealty to Bob's.

"I like things to be orderly," Lynch told the *New York Times*. "For seven years I ate at Bob's Big Boy. I would go at 2:30, after the lunch rush. I drank a chocolate shake and four, five, six, seven cups of coffee—with lots of sugar. And there's lots of sugar in that chocolate shake. It's a thick shake. In a silver goblet. I would get a rush from all this sugar, and I would get so many ideas! I would write them on these napkins. It was like I had a desk with paper. All I had to do was remember to bring my pen, but a waitress would give me one if I remembered to return it at the end of my stay. I got a lot of ideas at Bob's.".

MARILYN MONROE ON BOB

"Have you heard from Bob?" wondered Marilyn. "I hope so."

GARRISON KEILLOR'S LAKE WOBEGON BOBS: Bobism: An Inspirational Moment

Announcer: . . . now here's an inspirational moment with a man standing close to me on stage. Bob?
Bob: Hello, my name is Bob and I'm the founder of the religion that bears my name, Bobism. Actually a lot of Bobism comes from my wife Judy so I was thinking of naming it after her, but—I didn't because . . . they already have that.
And now, brought to you by the Central Bobist Temple in Rapid City, Bob discusses the central ideas of Bobism.
Bob: One of our basic ideas is that—the things you do in this life—it's going to come back to *you* in a way. I mean, that if you do bad stuff to people—it's like there's sort of—I don't know—whatever you want to call it—a balance to things. (PAUSE)
That's all?
Bob: That's about it for today.
You've just heard Bob, the founder of Bobism, brought to you by the Central Bobist Temple in Rapid City, explaining some of the . . . don't you people . . . your theology . . . don't you deal with the afterlife, the existence of God, the origin of the universe . . . ?
Bob: We're workin' on those. We're workin' on 'em.
Fine. Thanks Bob—from the Central Bobist Temple, explaining some of the principles of Bobism.
Bob: It's not easy being a founder of a whole religion you know.
For more information about the Bobist fair—
Bob: You think it's so easy, why don't you try it??? I don't see you startin' no religion!!! Huh???
Write to the Bobist Temple and not to this radio station.

—from *A Prairie Home Companion,* from American Public Radio
Copyright © 1987 Garrison Keillor. Reprinted by permission

PART TWO:

THE WORLD ACCORDING TO BOB

7

EXPLAINING THE BOB SURVEY

Bobs are borne out through hard evidence.

It is not enough to tell Bobs that they are a special breed: uncommonly supra-common in genus. Bobs, being Bobs, need proof. They must peer down on cold, empirical data before they will own up to their Bobness. This is to be expected. Besides, no one likes to be capriciously lumped into groups or stereotyped. Indeed, Bobs are above stereotyping—Bobs are prototypes. They are the genuine article. They are pure of spirit. Caprice has nothing to do with celebrating Bobs. Bobs, and *The Bob Book*, are based on true life.

Enter the Bob Survey.

The Bob Survey was created to show Bobs the Bobness of their ways.

Admittedly, the Bob Survey is a trick, a ploy, a calculated measure devised to lead Bobs down pathways of innermost reckoning. Bobs take no pleasure in plumbing their souls. Bobs don't tell all. Narcissism of this sort unnerves Bobs. But by

answering an array of simple and specific questions, Bobs can be found out. They emerge with clarity and sharpness. They bob to the surface, if you will. And in so doing, they unwittingly endorse the thesis that is *The Bob Book*—that is, they are alike in their Bobness. But then they have little choice in the matter.

Disallowed Survey Respondent: Bob The Weather Cat, of KTAU-Portland, Oregon.

WHO TOOK THE BOB SURVEY

Bobs. Only Bobs. Nobody but Bobs.

For a while, we debated over just who was qualified to complete the Bob Survey. Could, say, a Rob take the Bob Survey? No, we concluded, no Robs were allowed. They are pretenders, all too smooth for our purposes, and are best left out of literature altogether. Could a Roberta receive our questionnaire? No, we said, that would just be stupid. No Robins, either. Or Bobbys (unless they were at least part-time Bobs). Certainly no Bobbies. Roberts were invited, as long as they were Robert "Bobs" and, even so, we kept our eyes on them. Roberts are ultimately easy to spot—stuffy guys, mainly, who get fussy over question syntax and try to second-guess what the

Survey really means. Roberts are more trouble than they're worth.

We wanted Bobs. We got Bobs.

Hundreds of Bobs responded to a classified advertisement published in a popular national magazine. Others learned of the Bob Survey from news items, radio programs, and word of mouth that spread among the Bob brotherhood like brushfire. Many who sent in for Bob Surveys were not Bobs at all, but claimed they harbored aspirations of becoming Bobs. We politely turned them away. Bobs in every state of the union came forth, plus Canadian and British Bobs to boot. Two female Bobs turned up, both seeming quite Bob-like, but were not eligible to be factored into the Bob census. Dog and cat Bobs were submitted by several overly enthusiastic pet owners, who completed Bob Surveys on behalf of their well-named animals. Alas, only human Bobs needed apply. Bobs may be a bit predictable, but let's not get unnecessarily rude.

Every famous Bob was approached, the bounty of which is compiled in Part Three of this book. If there is a famous Bob whose Survey does not appear in *The Bob Book*, any of the following could be true: 1) The famous Bob has a humorless, overprotective secretary, agent, or manager, who never told Bob about it; 2) The famous Bob himself is humorless and aloof, and is thereby unworthy of being a Bob; or 3) The famous Bob is in the studio/on location making an album/film, and would really love to do it, but he's nowhere near a fax machine, and would we mind waiting until he finishes, which will be sometime late next year, probably before Arbor Day?

True Bobs found time. Most Bobs, after

all, are just happy to get a little attention.

HOW THE SURVEYS WERE TABULATED

The answers from all of the Bob Surveys were carefully collated, evaluated for pithy insight and telling traits, and finally used to construct the sociology of Bobs. The thoughts and proclivities of all Bobs surveyed informed every page of this book. Hundreds of the most wise and rueful Bob Survey responses—in Bobs' own words—are featured throughout the book. A master list of quoted Bobs matched to identification numbers appears in the back of the book, as The Bob Index.

THE BOB SURVEY MADE EASY

Here is what the Bob Survey looks like, as completed by a Bob.

For purposes of demonstration and explanation, *The Bob Book* called upon a Bob whom we knew and trusted—indeed, the father of one of the authors—to attack the Survey first.

The Bob Survey
Name: Bob Zehme
Residence: South Holland, Illinois.
Occupation: Florist.

KEY QUESTIONS:
A. Why did you stick with the name Bob, instead of Robert, Bobby, Robby, Rob, etc.?
The name fits the guy. When I write Robert on a check or official paper, it feels like another me.

B. What does it MEAN to be Bob?
Do the best you can with what you've got. Be fair and understanding. Do more than your share. Don't wait for thank-yous.

HOW YOU SEE THE WORLD:
1. What's your idea of a great weekend?
Do some outdoor/indoor chores. Watch a little sports on TV. Dinner, in or out. Go to movie or watch one on TV.

A: To put this question another way: Why are Bobs Bobs? Here, they are forced to acknowledge that they made a choice in life, then think about what led them down that path. A general sense of existentialist self-awareness always emerges in this answer, as well as displeasure with relatives who wrongheadedly insist on calling them Bobby.

B: This one makes Bobs nervous. It begs for Bobs to feel a little self-important—an unnatural act—and attempt near-high-minded postulation. Bobs reveal humility in their responses here, as well as an unwavering practicality regarding their roles in the cosmos. In truth, Bobs think ethos; they believe cosmos to have been a Marx brother.

1. How Bobs spend weekends should reveal the following: Our suspicion is that Bobs know exactly how to achieve to peace, whereas most others do not. Bobs find a formula for personal respite and adhere to it, never swerving into areas of experimentation and spontaneous exploration. It's not cautiousness as much as it is just knowing what works.

2. Are all Bobs good? Do Bobs notice other Bobs? Here, Bobs examine themselves as a breed and rack their brains to remember every Bob they've ever encountered. This question more than any other nudges Bobs, self-effacing or not, toward admiring the thesis of *The Bob Book*.

2. Have you ever met a Bob you didn't like? Explain.

No. All the Bobs I know are quiet, unassuming, honest, and just nice to know.

3. What's the handiest thing you do?

Gardening. Carpentry.

3. If things go wrong—tangible things, fixable things—Bobs lunge to correct them. Bobs are sturdy and self-reliant and this question explores the pride Bobs take in their ability to make things right. It also gauges practicality and self-confidence, with regard to their know-how.

4. What distinguishes Bobs from the society in which they dwell? What does Bob see in others that seems completely antithetical to his own being? How does Bob know that he's different from the pack? By owning up to what he dislikes, Bob essays his own doctrine of social ethics.

4. What kind of behavior in other people makes you uncomfortable?

Pushy. Braggadocios. Phony.

5. Describe your version of hell on earth.

Being indebted to someone, or having to beg for something.

5. Bob's hell is not such a very bad hell. Bob's hell is a practical hell, a hell Bob knows exactly how to avoid. The darkest recesses of Bob's soul aren't all that dark; Bobs are not fanciful about horror. Their horror is palpable and kind of innocent, as their responses here suggest.

6. How to measure a man's innate benevolence? Trust is the key. Bobs must assess the world that lurks outside of his own sphere and decide just whom he will allow in. Good sense is what will be displayed here; good Bob sense.

6. In whom do you trust? In whom don't you trust?

Trust: My wife and family. Most any Bob. Distrust: Anyone who offers a deal too good to be true. Some people bear watching.

7. What are the most important things you know about women?

Unpredictable. Volatile. Watch your step.

7. Women are not exactly Boblike. And this is good. But it is a disparity worth exploring. What sort of woman ends up with Bob? What sort of woman puts up with Bob? How does Bob relate to women?

8. If Bobs are the utilitarian souls we suspect them to be, what could better reflect their basic needs? What Bob needs most he keeps within reach. Here is what Bob needs and especially what he needs before drifting into the subconscious, a place Bob has always been less than enthused about, since it is difficult to get ball scores there.

8. What's on your nightstand?

Clock radio. Assorted magazines: *Money, Changing Times, Islands, Condé Nast Traveler.*

9. How much time each day do you spend on your hair? What look are you trying to achieve?

About twenty seconds. A quick brush and a shot of pump spray to batten down the few strands left. The Respectable Look.

9. Is Bob vain? Decidedly not. Here is just how not-vain Bob is, as reduced to the most specific time increment. Bobs don't work on their presentation as much as they are uniformly at one with it. This is why Bob looks like what Bob looks like. Un-concerned confidence is the issue.

10. What are you most comfortable wearing?

Old favorites.

10. Bobstyle continued: the unpretentious meter registers with astonishing precision here. Away from the expectations of business-world dress code, Bobs loosen up and find their natural element

11. Who or what did you want to grow up to be?

Successful.

11. How dreamy are Bob's aspirations. How lofty are Bob's loftiest goals? If Bob's feet are planted firmly on planet earth, just how far will he let his imagination run away with him? Our suspicion is that Bobs keep things simple and attainable.

12. What life philosophy should a father pass on to his children?

Always be good to your mother.

12. What do Bobs know for sure? If they have learned anything in life, here is where they will share it. Whatever has worked for them so far is clear to Bobs; if they have spawned offspring, these are the principles they will urge upon their progeny. Expect solid, tangible advice; that is, expect the expected.

FAVORITES:
BOOK: *Good Housekeeping Family Health and Medical Guide.*
MOVIE: *The Sound of Music.*
TV SHOW: *Sea Hunt.*
MAGAZINE: *National Geographic, Islands.*
BREAKFAST CEREAL: Grape-Nut Flakes.
CAR: Buick.
SONG: "My Way."
AFTER-SHAVE: None. They're all too sickly sweet.
SPORT: Baseball.
SANDWICH: Hamburger with grilled onions.
DRINK: Iced tea.
NEWS ANCHOR: Ted Koppel

FAVORITES: How simple are Bob's simple pleasures? Just as Bobs can always be counted on, here are the things in life that never disappoint Bobs. What is interesting to note is that Bobs make choices that have less to with passion than with sturdiness, dependability, and durability. Bob's favorites hold up well: solid cars, no-nonsense breakfast cereals, sandwiches without radicchio or honey-pesto mayonnaises. Bobs favor books that service rather than daunt or dazzle. Bobs need anchormen they can trust, not guys with great hair. Bobs get to the point and delight in the things that have a point, especially ingenious surveys for books based on shockingly obvious themes.

8 THE HANDY BOB

"If I can't swim or get exercise, I may end up building something or knocking down trees or clearing brush."

—BOB VILA

How many Bobs does it take to screw in a light bulb?

One, of course.

Bobs are devout utilitarians.

If things go wrong—tangible things, fixable things—Bobs lunge to correct them. Bobs are sturdy and self-reliant and delight in making things right.

Bobs fix. They repair, restore, recondition, revamp, remodel, and just plain tinker. Bobs putter famously. Now, it isn't as though others cannot do this stuff and even do it more proficiently. It's just that Bobs make it their business to know how things work. When things don't work, Bobs make it their business to know that too. It is a point of pride, essential to their self-worth.

Bobs do it themselves.

Often they do it badly. But they must try first. Bobs are at one with being flat on their backs, lying under the sink or the car or the house. Bobs like the view from below. They like to see the parts. They identify with the parts. They are the parts. Similarly, no chore is a chore to a Bob. A chore is a challenge, a gauntlet heaved, a sword drawn, an opportunity to bask in sweet, understated glory. Bobs are at ease with hard work. For them, to sweat is no sweat at all. Sawdust and grime are their second skin. Bobs look good dirty.

If Mr. Fixit had a first name, it would be Bob. If Mr. Goodwrench had a first name, it would be Bob. If celebrity handyman Bob Vila had a first name that wasn't Bob, it would either be a big mistake or have something to do with a federal witness relocation program.

Before any Bob can relinquish a project, Bobness forces him to plumb his resources. Or, at least, pause for a moment.

> "I can empty any beer products lying about or in the icebox."
> —BOB MOUND, chef

Indeed, instead of calling a plumber, Bobness forces Bob to take the first crack at a leaky faucet himself. Rather than hire the neighbor kid, Bobness impels Bob to mow his own lawn.

Bob could be stingy with his tools, but Bobness obliges Bob to loan them out—and complain only to his wife that he doesn't get them back.

Bobs derive more pleasure from assem-

> "I'm good with electronic equipment. With VCRs and computers. I know how they work."
> —BOB NEWHART

bling the patio furniture than from lounging in it. Bobs are more apt to plant the roses than to stop and smell them. Bobs would rather install the Malibu lighting than spend the day at Malibu. Bobs will try doing most anything that involves construction, erection, or installation, preferably without reading the instructions—though they will if they must, even if it means puzzling over the bad English translations.

Bobs relish turning any task into a triumph: garage-door openers, ceiling fans,

security systems, baby-sitting, satisfying the wife, making do with leftovers, and twisting animal shapes out of balloons. Bobs also reap great satisfaction from accurately reading maps, opening jars, and getting dressed for any occasion in under five minutes. Bobs instinctively know how to take a car engine apart and put it back

> *"I think I can do things I know I can't do and I keep repeating that same mistake."* —**BOB KEESHAN**

together again, especially if it is entirely unnecessary.

Once Bob gives it his best shot, even though he may have failed, he feels better just for having tried. This makes it easier for Bob to enjoy the self-satisfied glow— not to mention the well-deserved cold

> *"I can make something out of nothing and have it work."* —**BOB STORM, USAF**

brew or two—that only hands-on effort can bring. Bobs nap better in the afternoon knowing they've taken full responsibility.

Then they'll call for expert help. Bobs are nothing if not pragmatic.

> *"I'm handy at loaning out my tools."* —**BOB KENTON BROWN, sales**

WHAT BOBS DO BEST

• I'm an all-around handyman. I seek things out in need of repair. [129] Odd jobs around the house and yard. [115] • Open jars. [181] • Paint. [134] • Read maps. [109] • Play pool. [25] • I have an NRA sharpshooter rating with small-caliber pistols. [84] • Remember. [127] • I'm a virtual encyclopedia of useless information. [18] • Just about everything. [202] • Keep a VW running. [198] • Install ceiling fans, garage-door openers, and shelving. [161] • Remodeling. [64] • Wiring. [14] • Wallpapering. [44] • Woodworking. [121] • Work with my trees. I grow them from seed. [2] • Zoom around by wheelchair (I am a paraplegic). [151] • Trailer my boat and take it fishing. [160] • Skip tracing. [152] • Shovel snow, which is important because the wife won't and if I don't I'm stuck in the house. [154] • Solve problems. [187] • Take something apart, fix it, put it back together without plans. [177] • I can build anything you can draw. [150] • Gardening and bricklaying. [204] • Fix cassette tapes eaten by tape players. [15] • Fix the toilet. [158] • Hook up a VCR. [106] • Change motor oil. [103] • Build lava stone walls. [128] • Major repair work on high-performance autos. [23] • Repair bicycles. [10] • Masturbate, I guess. [162] • Stay out of the way of assholes. [210]

TALENTS OF THE MODERN BOB

• Fold napkins. [67] • Do my own laundry. [207] • Baby-sit my kids. [192] • Clean up after the rug rats. [190] • Sew. [yes, sew]. [3] • Grow organic elephant garlic. [80] • Make a great cheesecake. [167] • Whip up an incredible omelet at any time of the day for any of my inebriated friends. [194] • Keep my cool much longer than most people. [139] • Repair nuclear reactors. [108] Add quickly with a calculator. [8] • Push the dishwasher button on. [79] • Get dressed for any occasion in less than five minutes. [37] • Find someone else who is handy. [214] • Mow the lawn with a self-propelled mower. [97]

STUPID BOB TRICKS

• Alphabetize very rapidly. [22]
• Bite my toenails. [81]
• Build a pretty nice sand castle. [85]
• Mess up a room faster than anyone I know. [95]
• Turn everything and every situation into a joke. [96]
• Play *A-Team* theme through my nose. [54]
• Play the harmonica with my nose—while I eat. [125]
• Sing reggae music while doing a balance sheet. [124]
• Open a beer bottle with my teeth. [30]
• Make off-color comments. [100]
• Change flashlight batteries. [118]
• Make balloon animals. [31]
• Spin a basketball on my right index finger for great lengths of time. [104]
• Button my own shirt. [77]
• Unsnap any bra with two fingers. [146]

9 BOB'S GREAT WEEKEND

"Perfect weekend: rent a movie, eat some pizza, drink some pop, have my arm around a good-looking woman."

—BOB ENGSTROM, custodian

Bobs know exactly how to achieve peace, whereas most others do not.

It happens every weekend.

Bobs find a formula for personal respite and adhere to it, never swerving off into areas of experimentation and spontaneous exploration. It's not cautiousness as much as it is just knowing what works.

Bobs count on their weekends.

These are never haphazard affairs. Bob's days off are, instead, an assortment of simple aims and modest objectives. Bobs shun the fanciful, the flighty, the frivolous. Bobs would rather catch up on their chores than go to Paris for the weekend. (Paris, incidentally, is never high on Bob's vacation list. No place to water-ski.)

Bobs are incapable of wasting weekends. They know exactly what they are doing even when they are not doing anything. When Bobs do nothing, they do so because nothing is exactly

BOB OVERBOARD!

One weekend in 1989, just after 7:00 P.M., Bob Hutchinson fell off a sport-fishing boat into 64-degree waters halfway between Catalina Island and King Harbor Marina. Bob had been emptying a bait tank when the boat dipped suddenly, leaving Bob to bob in the ocean for nearly five hours. Bob refused to go under. "It was bad enough that I'd fallen over," he later told the *Los Angeles Times*. "I wasn't going to complicate things by dying."

Bob had been gone almost 20 minutes before anyone knew he was missing.

When Bob Beauchamp, the boat's pilot, discovered his complement was one man light, he searched for the missing Bob almost 4½ hours before being ordered to port by the Coast Guard. "It looked bleak," said the dry Bob, who wasn't ready to call it quits. "I didn't think I'd ever see Bob again."

He was wrong. Bob was out but not drowned. He found a buoy. He clung tight in the two-foot swells. Finally, a Coast Guard cutter crew heard Bob ringing the buoy bell over and over. Then he whistled a tune to bring them closer in the darkness. Bob did what he had to do. "I wanted to see my family again," he said. "I thought of my [three] children the most. I wanted to live.

"I was too embarrassed to die."

what they want to do. As such, they accomplish in spite of themselves. Easily achievable goals permit Bobs to feel dutiful even when at rest or play. But Bob's idea of play might as well be another man's idea of toil. Buoyed by responsibility when others might be burdened by it, Bobs seize the day every day. They are neither zealous nor slothful; rather they are chronically competent, even in matters of repose.

> *"A great weekend? Lying in the sun doing absolutely nothing."*
> **—BOB BARKER**

"I wanted to get a few things accomplished," Bob will recall over his first cup of Monday-morning java. "And I did." And visions of replaced doorknobs, newly installed spark plugs, and bags of lawn mulch might dance in his head. As we have seen in the previous chapter, Bobs get things done. Moreover, they consider relaxation and handiwork to be synonymous. For them, meditation is not unlike trimming the hedge. In fact, meditation *is* trimming the hedge. Bobs are lulled into sweet somnolence by the steady whir of power tools.

Home is where the Bob is on weekends, more or less. Bobs don't get away much; they just get comfortable. They find solace in their own backyards, literally. After a

> *"You don't have to go away. Bobs have fun when the people around them are having fun."*
> **—BOB HOWLEY, interior landscaper**

little yardwork, a snooze in the sun, or a splash in the pool, Bobs light charcoal, singe meat, consume beverages, watch athletics, and engage in convivial behavior. They avoid telephones and neckwear. If they are family men—and Bobs with families must be family men—Bobs attempt to remind family members of what they look like without work waiting, and especially what they look like while wearing stupid hats. Bobs love stupid hats. They look stupid wearing them. And thoroughly comfortable.

THE COMPLETE

THE BASIC BOB WEEKEND

- Any weekend is a good weekend. [157]
- To be outside on a warm, sunny day, doing just about anything—or nothing. [174]
- Sack in late. Football, boxing, heavy on the food. [138]
- Watching the Runnin' Rebels, yeah! [100]
- Playing cards and drinking Budweiser beer. [175]
- Pancakes for breakfast, steaks for dinner. [212]
- Women, tequila, golf. [17]
- Going to a Cubs game. [134]
- Attending the NCAA final four. [8]
- Friday—get loaded, go to Blue Oyster
  Cult concert
  Saturday—case of beer, rent some movies
  Sunday—watch football with the guys at
  the bar. [131]

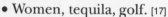

- Combine trout fishing with a nice motel
  and good restaurants. [121]
- To be alone with my wife, have a few wine
  coolers, watch good movie, and make love. [58]
- Going to the beach with my gal. [128]
- Having someone share my bed.
  Going to church. [44]
- Right now I am sitting in jail; a great weekend for me would be being home with my family. I was put in here for something stupid. [200]
- Staying in bed with my naked wife. [69]

THE RELUCTANT BOB WEEKEND

- I want a weekend free of responsibility and all the worries that come with it. [129]
- I like there to be nothing that I *have* to do. [156]
- I like to take my boat and disappear. [215]
- I don't want to hear anyone calling my name. [203]
- No phones, no TV, no jerks, no traffic, no worries. [3]
- No razors or shoes. [115]
- Nothing involving rooms full of strangers engaging in stupid-speak. [46]
- Not being bothered when I want to take a nap on the porch. [210]
- Having a 12-pack, locked doors, answering machine on, no lights, loud stereo. [214]
- Not being home to be friendly or to loan out my few remaining tools. [135]

BOB WEEKEND

THE PRODUCTIVE BOB WEEKEND

- Working in my shop. [5]
- Anything outdoors using my hands. [29]
- Screwing around on my computer. [49]
- Working in my garden. [50]
- Cutting my own firewood. [123]
- Working with my show cattle and fishing. [152]
- Catching up on sleep lost during the work week. [48]
- Efficient use of time, getting something done. [163]
- Achieving Monday is the usual goal. [51]

THE FANTASY BOB WEEKEND

- Young women, case of beer, no phone. [111]
- Winning thc Ncw York State lottery drawing on a Saturday night. [77]
- The Dodgers beating the Giants with Vin Scully at the mike. [57]
- Flying to a major-league baseball city to take in a weekend of games. [4]
- Have Harmon Killebrew, Kirby Puckett, Rod Carew, and a few other average guys drop over and discuss world events. [118]
- Driving to Memphis for ribs. [18]
- Doing a music gig in a happening lounge in a tropical paradise. [181]
- Going to dinner and not having to pay. [32]
- Plane trip to Vegas and coming back a winner. [144]
- Las Vegas; shrimp scampi; Scandinavian twin sisters. [125]
- Me, two girls, and 58 yards of Jell-O. [159]
- Great and repeated sex in which ecstasy is not faked. [196]
- Hiring someone else to cut the lawn. [161]

10 WHAT MAKES

"I want to know what a person wants, where he plans on going, and how he plans on getting it and getting there. If someone is mysterious or I can't figure them out, I get upset."

—BOB BOLYARD, secretary

Bobs are solid and expect solidness from others.

Unfortunately, the universe is suffused with much gas and liquid. Which means that Bobs are forced to contend with blowhards and gushers, with overheated windbags and slippery cons, with empty sacks and wet noodles.

Bobs hate time wasted. This is the essential Bob truth.

All else is secondary.

What rankles Bobs most is behavior that convolutes an easily made point. Bobs hate garnish. Bobs want it straight. They want it unadorned. They want it now. For this reason, if Bobs ruled the world, weekends would begin on Thursdays. Not because Bobs are slothful; on the contrary, we already know that Bobs live to accomplish goals. If our society was peopled with Bobs and only Bobs, who would there be to impede progress? Why would a work week require more than four days? And think of the money that could be saved on business cards. True, there would be some problem in getting dates for Saturday nights. And

BOB SQUIRM?

there would, of course, be no more French food. Still, it's an idea worth pondering.

The key is directness.

Here is how to make Bobs happy, in social scenarios: Tell them what you want. Tell them what you think. Don't tell them what they want, or what you think they want to hear, or what you don't really want or think but you're too timid to tell the truth. Say what you mean, always. If you don't know what you mean, say nothing. Or else say that you don't know what you mean, if that's what you mean.

Don't pretend to know a Bob better than you really do. Never try to impress a Bob. Do not regale Bobs with stories that have no point or stories whose point is to make a Bob think you're special. Bobs have nothing to prove and feel you don't either. Demean no one in the presence of Bobs. And never suck up to a Bob. Never compliment Bobs on their ties—they know better and so do you. Look Bobs squarely in the eye—but never for too long, since this will make Bobs nervous. Along these same lines, avoid gratuitous touching to underscore your conversations. Bobs don't want you to touch them, unless you are a woman, and even then, it had better be the real thing and not some phony cocktail-party sort of behavior.

> *"I can't stand people who never relax, talk too much, talk loud, know everything, chew with their mouths open, lick their fingers, and are dirty."* —**BOB STORM, USAF**

DENTAL HEALTH *adviser*

Hi, my name is Bob, and I'm a tooth-Grinder

- The Stress Connection
- The Extent of the Damage
- Ways to Find Relief

Tooth-Grinders Anonymous

Don't invade Bobspace. Stand three feet back and keep it that way. Don't pry; Bobs will tell you all you need to know about themselves, and maybe even a little bit more, since Bobs haven't all that much to hide. Never share idle gossip with Bobs; they just don't care, and in their opinion, neither should you. Don't argue in front of Bobs (although you may certainly argue with them); few things embarrass Bobs more than having to witness public quarreling, especially between couples. (Bobs firmly believe squabbling of this nature should be reserved for the ride home in the car.) Also, Bobs hate fake accents. Don't even try fooling a Bob. Just be yourself; after all, it's only Bob.

HOW TO DEAL WITH BOBS: 15 SIMPLE RULES

- Don't waste my time. [163]
- Don't say, "Where have I seen you before?" [87]
- Don't fail to give me a firm handshake. [47]
- Don't talk about something you know I don't care about. [61]
- Don't assume you know what I'm thinking. How the hell would you know, anyway? [213]
- Don't try to convince me to do it your way long after I've made up my own mind. [151]
- Don't butt in. [14]
- Don't think you know more than I do. [81]
- Don't tell stories that have no point or say "um" a lot. [214]
- Don't gossip over petty incidents. [144]
- Don't stare at me. [219]
- Don't come to visit and never leave. [82]
- Don't pretend to be really good friends of mine in front of other people. [68]
- Don't tell me to smile. [106]
- Females: Please, don't say no. [124]

MARCY DROGIN PRESENTS

BOB'S SELF - IMPROVEMENT SEMINAR

A NEW COMEDY

HELP US HELP BOB...

IT'S $8.00

WHAT BOBS HATE MOST: UP CLOSE & PERSONAL

- When a person gets right in my face to talk to me. [91]
- Nosy questions about my personal life. [152]
- People who invade my space and don't back off when they're asked to. [158]
- Mimes, especially in elevators. [185]
- Animated conversations within three or four inches of my face. [140]
- People who touch me the entire time they're talking to me. [145]
- Standing closer than six inches to me while talking. [10]
- Encroachment, either spiritual or physical. [28]
- "Get your clammy hands off of me!" [18]

BOB'S PET PEEVES

- Lovers' quarrels in public. [181]
- When people talk with food in their mouths. [10]
- Women chewing gum or anyone eating with their mouth open. [anon]
- Public displays of affection; eating in grocery stores. [134]
- Excessive behavior of any kind, instant intimacy, and public drunkenness. [22]
- Overly crude behavior. Curt and cheap conversation. [anon]
- Pushy newspaper boys and Jehovah's Witnesses. [190]
- People who can't sit still. [131]
- Wiggling feet. [142]
- Wimpiness and indecisiveness. [108]
- Inconsistency. [117]
- Fence riders and no-opinion bastards. [195]
- Sycophantic, foolish, egoistic, predatory, and boorish behavior. [21]
- Swaggering by men under five feet eight inches tall. [84]
- People who are too hip to be happy. [156]
- Being judgmental. [15]
- No human being is entitled to arrogance. [37]
- There is a difference between cockiness and confidence. [59]
- People who argue over nothing. [128]
- False chumminess and familiarity. [198]
- Corporate kissers. [33]
- Conformists. [57]
- Laziness and irresponsibility. People who think things are owed to them. [157]
- Lying. [66]
- A person who will slit your throat for a dollar. [95]

BOB ACROSS

He's in it for Bob.

He spread the word, and the word was Bob.

He took Bob across America.

When Bob Manley, a 25-year-old photographer and art-school student, contemplated what would be his final show before graduating from the California Institute for the Arts, he found inspiration in his mirror.

Bob.

So Bob spent a semester taking pictures of Bob. He gave his camera to people as they passed him in the school hallways and said, "Take a picture of me." Soon he enlarged 15 photos of himself, dressed in a variety of styles, and mounted them on pedestals. They were taller than Bob, who stood six-one. "I've always wanted to be taller," he said.

He installed his Bobs in a gallery space. He hung a sign that read, "Picture yourself with the Bob of your choice," and people posed with "Bob" in front of a color mural of an ocean breaking.

He called it *The Bob Show.*

Later, he just called it *Bob.*

The exhibition was a great success, and Bob's public demanded an encore. For *Bob II*, Bob's enlarged personal effects (deodorant, brush, comb, tie, shirt, hat) were mounted on pedestals. On one wall hung a 14-by-9-foot head shot of Bob.

When it was all over, Bob did what no other Bob would do—which was only reasonable since apparently no other Bob has ever done what Bob did in

AMERICA: A QUEST

the first place: Bob took himself and all 15 of his likenesses on the road. He piled his Bob dreams into a 1977 Olds Cutlass, which pulled a specially designed trailer emblazoned with the legend "Bob Across America." One Bob likeness rode in back: Backseat Bob. Eventually, the other Bobs were also named: Canyon Bob, Vegas Bob, Traveling Bob, Miami Bob, Mullet Bob, Adventure Bob.

He called the odyssey *Bob Across America*.

Bob and his co-pilot, his cousin Dan, departed from Venice, California, on July 4, 1988. Their journey lasted 4½ months and covered thousands of miles. They visited over 100 cities and 60 small towns in 41 states. They spent six weeks in Miami and six weeks in Boston. They had major car trouble in Washington State. They sold some "Bob Across America" T-shirts. They took thousands of photos. People everywhere clamored to be in a picture with the Bob of their choice. Bob got newspaper coverage. One Bob [photographic] wearing a parachute, was pushed from an airplane, and landed intact. Another explored scenic Carlsbad Caverns. Another dived five fathoms to visit Jules Underseas Lodge, the world's only underwater motel. Vegas Bob gambled in Las Vegas.

"Yessiree BOB," Manley would later remark, and then include the remark in his press kit.

Bob has also had this to say about his adventures: "I don't want people to come away thinking I'm egotistical. I'm just an average guy."

The trip cost Bob about $10,000. "I've invested my life savings in this," Bob told the *Los Angeles Times*. "When I get back, I'm going to be penniless, homeless, and jobless."

But at least he's not shy anymore, as our interview with him suggests.

Would your project have worked if your name had been Fred?
No. I couldn't have had a T-shirt that said "Fred Across America." There's definitely something to the name Bob. I've thought about that for a long time.

Who was more Bob-like—you or your cut-out characters?
I'm my own Bob; the characters became another Bob. Both as much Bob as Bob can be. I thought that the characters were becoming a representation of all Bobs, maybe.

How did Bobs who came to the show react?
Whenever I ran into a Bob, they just wanted to be part of it; they wanted to have their picture taken with Bob and to get their T-shirt and pin. It was only three or four years ago that I discovered that being a Bob was somebody special. I didn't realize it. In fact, I resisted being called Bob for a long time. I wanted to be called Robert. Through enormous pressure from friends and family, it ended up being Bob. People just insisted that that was going to be my name. I had no choice in the matter. So I just accepted that I was Bob and [smiles] discovered that was fine.

11 BOB IN HELL

"Hell on earth is sitting beside loud, boring, self-centered, egotistical people at a formal dinner party, with too many utensils." —BOB DENVER

Bob's hell is not such a very bad hell.

When Bobs imagine their versions of hell on earth, they do not conjure up atrocity. They do not hear teeth gnashing and feel flesh seared and taste the tang of their own blood. Bobs are not fanciful about horror. The darkest recesses of Bob's soul are not all that dark. Horror for Bobs tends to be of a palpable, everyday nature, almost innocent in kind. Like being forced to listen to Barbra Streisand albums. Or do some public speaking.

Bob's hell is a practical hell, a hell Bob knows exactly how to avoid.

Hell for Bobs is being stuck. Being stuck derails Bobs from getting things done and getting things done is what Bobs are all about. It is an impediment that vexes Bobs most, coagulating into a mire that bogs Bob's easy existence. Bobs loathe being at the mercy of others. Bobs do not like their self-sufficiency challenged and their free will compromised. Bobs like to be left to their own devices, but aren't crazy about being left alone, espe-

THE FAR SIDE — By GARY LARSON

CONGRATULATIONS
BOB
TORTURER
OF THE MONTH

BOB'S BIGGEST FEARS

- Nothing but women's sports on TV. [203]
- Singing solo in public. [74]
- Going to the dentist. [2]
- Doing nothing. [169]
- Being broke and ill. [90]
- Finding a killed road animal in your bed. [85]
- Running out of butts and having no cash. [82]
- Sitting in a crowded room. [68]
- A tax audit. [198]
- Being yelled at by a woman. [136]
- Accordion playing and drum solos. [133]
- Being in an elevator with the girl of my dreams and two huge guys with tremendous body odor and her thinking it's me who smells. [155]
- A day with my ex-wife. [64]
- Anyplace with no food or TV. [130]
- Being alone. [152]
- Being fat, ugly, stupid, and named Kevin. [159]
- Being without Vivian. [183]

"Hell is if Anheuser Busch goes out of business."
—**BOB RENNA**, textile cutter

"Hell is living with a clown."
—**BOB JONES**, salesman

"Hell is not making quota."
—**BOB KANARICK**, marketing manager

cially without beer, or money to pay for beer, or a bottle opener with which to free beer from its squalid confinement.

Bobs implicitly make the most of a bad situation, which may be why their worst nightmares always come with escape routes. For instance, most Bobs revile formality. But they will navigate such narrow straits on their own terms. In stuffy restaurants, a Bob may not always know his salad fork from his dinner fork, but he will never be afraid to mention it.

Limit a Bob, though, and you will defeat him, for Bobs limit themselves at the outset more than any other sort would have the good sense to do. It's what makes them Bobs, ultimately.

BOB'S ULTIMATE INDIGNITIES

- Running out of beer. [108]
- Not being able to work. [177]
- No competition. [63]
- Tailgating at Milwaukee County Stadium and forgetting the beer and brats. [81]
- No ballgames, no old Chevies, no talk radio late at night. [69]
- No cable TV and a hard sofa. [96]
- Living with a woman who nags and bosses and won't accept me for myself unconditionally, especially if she has violent tendencies. [181]
- Having my mother-in-law move in with me. [114]
- No women, beer, cars. [25]
- Three Bobs in a group of four. [87]
- Not having control of the TV remote. [167]
- A whole week without my computer. [49]
- Living in Bel Air while working as a high-powered entertainment executive. [5]
- A case of imported beer with no bottle opener. [131]

BOB'S HELL TRAPS

- Changing diapers for a living. [53]
- Sitting in a dentist's waiting room next to a very pushy born-again Christian. [145]
- A room with nothing to read and the only other person there a religious nut. [22]
- Being trapped on a Muzak-equipped elevator with six attorneys discussing comparative country clubs. [45]
- Waiting in a long line with all lawyers and insurance men. [157]
- Being at a party when two or more ex-girlfriends are in the room. [119]
- To drive for an eternity with no radio. [93]
- Taking a trip from Florida to Detroit on Greyhound. [35]
- Driving across California in a Chevette with a chain-smoker. [86]
- To be enclosed in a small area that's real dark and not be able to get out right away. [180]
- Occupying the middle seat on a three-across row on a cross-country flight. [37]
- A long flight next to a tedious, talkative person. [208]
- Being locked in a room with guys named Troy, Keiffer, Brenton, and Xavier. [10]
- To be locked in a closet inside Pee Wee's Playhouse. [19]
- Sharing a cell with Phil Donahue. [30]
- Being at a party with only Tammy Faye Bakker, Senator Strom Thurmond, and Jerry Falwell, and contracting acute laryngitis. [162]
- Being stranded on a desert island with the entire Van Patten family. [32]
- Being landlocked with no potential for aquatic activity. [140]
- Living in Utah. [100]
- Jail/prison. I've seen it and it's not a pretty sight. [125]
- Being forced to live with my parents for the rest of my life. [91]
- Living with my mother. [116]
- Being stuck in a relationship with a female who's vindictive, and violent. [147]
- Being stuck in a room with no windows or doors, with a Nebraskan. [137]
- Being stuck in a room with 200 women chewing gum with their mouths open. [43]
- Being in stuck in an airport overnight. [109]
- Being stuck in the left lane doing 35 mph when there is no traffic except for three cars around you. [95]
- Being dropped in a crowd of Yuppies. [52]
- Having to live in a big city. [47]
- Marriage. [206]

TO HELL AND BACK, THE STORY OF DR. BOB'S HISTORIC BATTLE

Dr. Bob was a sober Bob. He was, in fact, the Bob most famous for his sobriety. This was not always so. Before Dr. Bob was sober, he was frequently inebriated. But let's not get ahead of ourselves.

Dr. Bob—whose given name was Robert Holbrook Smith—co-founded Alcoholics Anonymous in 1935, which is why he will forever be known as Dr. Bob and not Robert Holbrook Smith. Dr. Bob actually suited him best, for he was a man who essayed decency, self-discipline, and simplicity. Also, he liked the outdoors and Buicks. He took his first nip at age nine: hard apple cider stashed in a bale of hay. He dried out at age 46 in Akron, Ohio, where he practiced as a rectal surgeon. Never one to indulge in deep introspection, he tended to explain his alcoholism almost offhandedly: "I just loved my grog," he would say, and that would be that.

As such, the Bob-like traits of Dr. Bob are textbook in nature. In the biography, *Dr. Bob and the Good Old-Timers*, whose author is, natch, anonymous, we learn of his preternatural calmness, his practicality under pressure, his extremely large hands, and his fondness for wiseguy slang. As for the latter, it was not uncommon for Dr. Bob to recall large meals he had ingested with statements like, "Well, we put on the nosebag yesterday." Such was his antic charm.

"He kept it simple," said Betty B, who worked with Dr. Bob as a student nurse at the City Hospital of Akron. "His surgical skills were admired by nurses and doctors alike, yet he used fewer instruments and other operating paraphernalia than any other surgeon. Most surgeons are prima donnas. They have temper tantrums and they throw instruments. [But] the rougher the going, the more calm Dr. Bob became.

Still, Dr. Bob knew when to get tough.

Nurse Betty recalled the way he admonished interns who lackadaisically prepped patients before rectal surgery: "I'll always remember Dr. Bob saying, 'How the hell would you like someone pulling hairs out of your ass?' Yes, he was blunt. But there was nothing cross or phony about the man. He was just a real guy."

Bill Wilson, known in legend as Bill W, delivered Dr. Bob from drink. To quell hangovers, he would load Bob up with a mixture of tomato juice, sauerkraut, and Karo corn syrup. On June 10, 1935, Bob declared himself permanently sober; this is acknowledged as the birthdate of Alcoholics Anonymous.

Dr. Bob's role as AA forefather only became public knowledge when it was mentioned in his wife's obituary, published upon her death in 1949. Dr. Bob lived for another year in his modest Akron home at 855 Ardmore, which was declared a national landmark in 1985 and now serves as a Dr. Bob museum (the office phone is answered, "Dr. Bob's!"). In the final year of his life, Dr. Bob happily kept to a steady diet of his favorite dish, meat loaf. "If he could have had his way," his housekeeper later lamented, "he would have had meat loaf every day of the week." Before his death from cancer on November 16, 1950, Dr. Bob forbade his AA colleagues from building a monument to his memory. He believed he had done nothing special and wanted to be remembered that way.

As an AA associate known only as Henrietta would note, "Bob had a strong character—like the Rock of Gibraltar. He never spoke as a founder. He always said, 'I just work here.'"

12 BOB'S DREAMS

"You reach a certain place and that's sufficient. You get your territory and you're content with that." —BOB DYLAN

Nosirree, Bob.

There is an inherent defeatism to being a Bob. So much so that Bob is the only name ever appended to the dour negative, "Nosirree." Never do we hear, "Nosirree, Roberto," or "Nosirree, Biff." Only Bobs are comfortable taking on this mantle of gloom. But then Bobs do tend toward unforgiving realism. Ask a Bob if he perceives life to be full of outlandish possibilities and he will reply, "Nosirree, Bob."

Bobs don't shoot for the stars.

Bobs keep their feet firmly planted on planet earth and tether their dreams accordingly. Bob's loftiest goals are rarely very lofty. A Bob will pin his hopes only to what is attainable, not to what is fantastic. He will cling steadfastly to the achievable. Bobs do not want to rule the world or live in a castle or build an underwater shopping mall; they want regular pay for regular work that they do awfully well. For the most part, Bobs want to grow up to be something they actually *can* grow up to be. In this way, they manage to avoid setting themselves up for a life of disappointment and despair. Why yearn to become president when your odds are obviously lousy? Who needs this

> *"I just wanted to do something very pragmatic, with a weekly check."*
> —BOB NEWHART

kind of pressure? Not Bobs. Nosirree.

Do not presume, however, to think that

Bobs settle for less. For Bobs, less is enough. Less is fine. Less is more than they ever hoped for. Besides, less is life. Bobs know this implicitly. Bobs don't need to aspire to delirious heights. Their self-esteem supports them no matter where they land. Should things not go exactly as planned, there is little anguish and regret. Bobs just seem to accept where life leads and try to do the best they can under the circumstances.

The Bob Survey demonstrates the sly vagaries of Bob dream-versus-reality pat-

THE FAR SIDE   By GARY LARSON

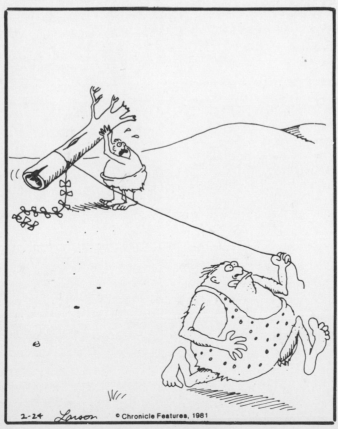

2-24 Larson © Chronicle Features, 1981

Okay, Bob! Go! Go!

"All of us, at one time or another, have wanted to be Buddhist monks, but, face it, Bob, you're an accountant."

"I've always wanted to work for the railroad, like my dad."
—**BOB DEMBROSKI,** railroad car man

terns, with startling results. For instance, Bob Newhart began his career as an accountant before turning comedian. Survey respondent Bob Ficenec wanted to be a stand-up comedian. Today he's an accountant. Bob Mair wanted to be a big reggae singer. Today he's a reggae-singing accountant. Bob Levatino wanted to be Buddy Rich, Mickey Mantle, or Paul McCartney. Today he's an accounting manager. It serves him right. Bob Wiren *wanted* to be an accountant. Today he's a hairdresser.

GO **BOB**-ING FOR FUN EVERY MORNING.

NEW SHOW!

Host: **BOB** Goen 9 AM

BLACKOUT

Host: **BOB** Eubanks 9:30

THE NEW **CARD SHARKS**

Host: **BOB** Barker 10 AM

THE **PRICE IS RIGHT**

WEEKDAYS! CBS⊙2

Special BoB Survey!

BOB WINCHESTER: WILD BOB
Domino's Pizza Deliverer
Murray, Kentucky

This Bob is a young collegian with an unbridled enthusiasm for life we at *The Bob Book* cannot help but admire. He will grow. He will learn. But, for now, he should be watched closely.

WHY I'M BOB: Because it made me feel heroic. It gives me a feeling of dignity and makes me want to conquer the world.

WHAT BEING BOB MEANS: It is the greatest thing in the world. As a matter of fact, I believe that the first man created was not an Adam but a Bob. Having this name is an honor in itself, but I make it even better.

MY GREAT WEEKEND: Going to parties and getting totally trashed while eating Domino's pizza.

BAD BOBS I'VE KNOWN: All Bobs are great, no matter how ignorant they are.

I'M HANDY AT...: Delivering pizzas and being a Sig Ep.

BEHAVIOR I DISLIKE: When people think they are as cool, calm, and collected as I am but they are really total assholes!

MY HELL ON EARTH: Having to be a PIKE (Pi Kappa Alpha Fraternity).

WHO I TRUST AND DISTRUST: I trust all Bobs and Sig Eps and all Domino's workers.

MOST IMPORTANT THING TO KNOW ABOUT WOMEN: How to get them drunk and keep them from becoming pregnant.

ON MY NIGHTSTAND: A lime-mist cooler, a box of rubbers, and the latest issue of *Playboy*.

TIME ON MY HAIR/MY LOOK: 15 minutes/the official Bob look.

COMFORTWEAR: Jeans and a sweatshirt.

BOYHOOD DREAM: To be any guy who has lots of gorgeous women hanging around him.

FAVORITES:
BOOK: *Animal Farm*.
MOVIE: *Die Hard*.
TV SHOW: *The Cosby Show*.
MAGAZINE: *Playboy*.
CEREAL: Lucky Charms.
CAR: Mazda Miata.
AFTER-SHAVE: Stetson.
SPORT: Basketball.
SANDWICH: Ham with cheese.
DRINK: Coke Classic.

WHAT BOBS WANTED TO BE WHEN THEY GREW UP

- Older. [87]
- Park ranger. [27]
- Physicist. [21]
- Truck or bus driver. [14]
- Pro football player. [204]
- Fry cook. [167]
- Owner of the largest chain of restaurants in the United States. [59]
- Sportscaster. [165]
- Sex and sleep therapist. [17]
- Professional trumpet player. [95]
- Game-show host. [32]
- Jet pilot. [210]
- Disc jockey. [66]
- Dentist, after my father. [197]
- Forester or geologist. [50]
- Baseball pitcher. [2]
- Astronaut. [115]
- Astronomer. [161]
- Detective. [72]
- Garbageman. [114]
- Policeman, but they don't get paid enough to do that kind of work. [70]
- Iron worker. [195]
- Hard-hat deep-sea diver. [128]
- Banker. [60]
- College professor. [28]
- Do voices for cartoons. [106]
- Known for leaving behind something worthwhile. [29]

ASPIRING TO BOB: BOBS WHO SING AND AREN'T REALLY BOBS

The Bobs are a singing group made up of five people none of whom is named Bob. (Each of them, however, has made it his or her middle name.) The Bobs sing a capella. That means nobody plays any instruments. For this feat, they have gotten to record four swell albums and earned a Grammy nomination. They are especially beloved in Italy, although they come from Berkeley. "Without the Bobs," their press release reads, "life as we know it on this planet would cease altogether and we would be plunged into unimaginable darkness." The Bobs are Gunnar Bob Madsen, Matthew Bob Stull, Richard Bob Greene, Janie Bob Scott, and Joe Bob Finetti, and there is nothing we can do about it.

How did you come to be Bobs?

MATTHEW BOB: One story has it that Richard was watching the Westminster Dog Show and heard the commentator say, "This dog was Bob the last three years." He found out it meant Best of Breed. B-O-B. Thus, inspiration. But it's an apocryphal story.

The truth: In the beginning, we were called the Oral Bobs, and somebody who saw our poster decided to shorten it for us.

But why Bob at all? What drew you to Bob?

GUNNAR BOB: It projects an easy familiarity—a whole group of easygoing regular guys (and a gal),

folks with whom you could go fishing or bowling or even to a boring opera. Most people would have a lot in common with a group of folks called The Bobs.

MATTHEW BOB: We had the name before we could think about the meaning.

Do you think your music appeals to real Bobs? Could The Bobs be too, um, esoteric for Bobs to appreciate?

MATTHEW BOB: We had one audience that was named Bob—they were all Bobs. Belonged to some Bob club.

JANIE BOB: Onstage, we do look like we'd be some really strange artsy kinda people. But we're just regular.

GUNNAR BOB: We do not use the name Bob in vain. Our simple unadulterated a capella singing would not only appeal to any true Bob, but is most probably practiced by the majority of Bobs in their showers.

RICHARD BOB: With no instruments, ours is do-it-yourself music. We're the Bob Vilas of music.

Would you consider legally affixing Bob to your name?

RB: Nah. We've used the name for more than seven years. That makes us common-law Bobs already, anyway.

13

BOBSTYLE

"Give me old clothes."
—BOB EVANS, sausage king

"I can't stand people whose hair is perfect." —BOB ESTES, salesman

Bobs come as they are.

They just don't care.

With Bobs, nothing is vanity, all is fair. If Bobs don't look good, they at least look okay. They look easy. They look like Bobs. We have gazed upon many a Bob—frankly, more of them than any Bob would care to hear about—and we can therefore issue such glib generalizations with resounding authority. We can safely conclude, for instance, that Bobs never look *fabulous*. Bobs do not sparkle. They do not glimmer. They do not require stares. Bobs do, however, make do. They make an appearance. They show up. Yet this should be enough and, in cases of large social functions, more than anyone has a right to expect of a Bob.

Bobs are neither slovenly nor are they slick. They possess a style that would not precisely qualify as style, as we know it. Bobstyle emerges by default. It emerges without forethought or deliberation. Bobs don't work on their presentation as much as they are uniformly at one with it. Mirrors mean little to Bobs; the

"Honey Where's My Bob Tie?"

view, they feel, is sort of unimpressive. Bobs just accept what the man upstairs has given them to work with—and in certain urban areas, that is more than likely to mean power tools on loan.

BOBWEAR

Clothes do not make the Bob.

Never do Bobs consider their wardrobe to be decoration. Clothes for Bobs are a practical consideration, not a fashion-driven one. Bobs rarely buy clothes because they *want* to; they do so because the alternative is to walk around naked. Bobs *can* dress well, but they are incapable of being dressed up. On a Bob, an expensive suit looks like a nice suit; remarkably, however, a cheap suit on a Bob also looks like a nice suit, unless it is plaid. Bobs never rely on their attire to make statements. Bobs speak for themselves (and even then, it helps if they are spoken to first).

As with most matters, Bobs find what works for them sartorially and cleave to it. Bobs look for formulas in haberdashery. They adopt uniforms. Their clothes must be old friends, not new acquaintances.

"I prefer to wear something with memories." —BOB DENVER

91

THE FAR SIDE   By GARY LARSON

"Listen! Just follow our distress beacon and send some help! ... We're in quadrant 57 of the Milky Way — on a planet called 'Bob's Shoeworld.'"

There must be no constricting cuts, no monogrammed pockets, no obtrusive de-

> *"If you were to see my hair coming, you'd say, 'Hey, that's Bob's hair.' "*
> **—BOB DEARBORN, broadcaster**

signer labels, and no caftans. Ascots and berets will never be tolerated. Bobs don't wear leather pants and worry about men who do.

Away from the expectations of workaday

> *"I've never combed or brushed my hair and I tend to scoff at men who do."* **—BOB BALLOU, consultant**

dress codes, Bobs find their natural element. The Bob Survey suggests that Bobs overwhelmingly favor jeans and chinos and T-shirts and ratty sweaters and beat-up shoes and baseball caps. Bobs, incidentally, seem to hate after-shave. Their preferred splash-on: water. Their preferred scent: Bob.

THE SMELL OF BOB: BOB'S FAVORITE AFTERSHAVES

BOB HOPE:	Hot water. Then cold water.
BOB NEWHART:	None.
BOB WELCH (Pitcher):	Old Spice.
BOB BARKER:	Mercurochrome.
BOB "SUPER DAVE" EINSTEIN:	I don't need any.
BOB DENVER:	None.
BOB FELLER:	Witch Hazel.
BOB MACKIE:	Never use it.
BOB GUCCIONE, JR.:	None.
BOB GOULET:	Sea Breeze.
BUFFALO BOB SMITH:	Mennen Skin Bracer.
BOB McGRATH:	None.
BOB COSTAS:	Old Spice, "like a real man."
BOB SAGET:	Sea Breeze.
BOB KEESHAN:	Nah, not really.

THE LOOK OF BOB: WHAT BOBS WOULD RATHER WEAR

BOB MATHIAS:	Work clothes.
BOB WELCH (Pitcher):	Nothing or shorts.
BOB WEATHERWAX:	Levi's, T-shirts.
BOB VILA:	Khakis and a sweater.
BOB URICH:	Sweat clothes.
BOB SAGET:	T-shirts and running pants.
BOB WELCH (Musician):	Cutoffs and no shoes.
BOB RICHARDS:	T-shirts. Levi's.
BOB NEWHART:	Cords and a golf shirt.
GOVERNOR BOB MILLER:	Levi's and golf shirts.
BOB McGRATH:	Work clothes and a wedding ring.
BOB MACKIE:	Sweatshirt and khakis.
BOB KEESHAN:	Chinos and sports shirt.
BOB GALE:	Blue jeans and T-shirts.
BOB KANE:	Old clothing.
BOB HOPE:	Cords and a golf shirt.
BOB MOULD:	Nondescript clothing.
BOB GOULET:	Jeans and sweater.
BOB FELLER:	Work shirt and work pants.

DAPPER BOB, TV HOST

Bob, pictured here, is a stylishly casual television star in Chicago. Like many television performers, Bob has a cardboard personality. Unlike his peers, however, Bob actually is cardboard. Since 1978, Bob has appeared at the outset of WTTW's *Image Union*, a local public television showcase of eclectic independent short films. Bob, in a superimposed state, strolls through precarious situations—on-rushing traffic, for instance—with easy grace and unwavering confidence, thereby meriting his name.

Bob's origins are sketchy, but then so is Bob. Here's Bob's story as told by co-producer Tom Weinberg:

"Bob is Mr. Everybody. We originally wanted to call him Mr. Man. He became Bob only after we got to know him.

"Bob was originally drawn and conceived by Jane Aaron, now an animator with world-class credentials. Bob had that star quality from the first frame…that smile, that twinkle, the inoffensive flat personality—what a guy! Some modern-art mavens have actually called us to ask, 'Is that *Image Union* man a Folon?' We smile and say, 'No, it's just Bob.'

"Why Bob?

"Well, he couldn't be anyone else. Had to be the same front and back. Couldn't be too much of anything. And he had to be nice but not a pushover. Bob. That's all.

"I would venture that Bob is better known locally in Chicago than the superintendent of schools, the senior senator from Illinois, or any congressmen.

"Bob has been on TV twice a week, every week since 1978. That's not quite Johnny Carson, but it *is* more than 1,300 appearances (plus promos). And he hasn't aged a bit—although the latest version seems to have a bit less hair."

BOB HAIR

There isn't much to say about Bob hair.

But then there doesn't seem to be much Bob hair about which to say much. This, of course, is thoroughly in keeping with the minimalism that is the Bob philosophy.

Bobs are born with little hair, and being Bobs, they seem to embrace the continuity of this look. Many Bobs bald. They bald all of their lives. Their hairlines recede and retreat and winnow, which permits Bobs to make self-deprecating hair jokes, ad nauseam. Bobs are almost proud of their hairlessness. Being bald, they secretly think (even if they are not bald), is better than having perfect hair. Men with perfect hair are the antithesis of Bobs.

If Bobs possess fruitful follicles, they let their hair do whatever it wishes, more or less. Bob hair behaves with Bob ease. Bob hair is unconcerned with itself. It is neither unruly nor is it daunting. It is Bob's crown of simplicity, his pelt of the ordinary. It is all muss, no fuss. If Bob hair could speak, it would say, "Who are you kidding? Don't even think about it. Really, just get out of here." Bobs know this and are therefore terrible at preening. They have no patience for it.

Because there is no greater measure of a man's vanity than the length of time he spends on his hair, the Bob Survey begged for the Bob truth. It turns out that Bobs spend, on average, 5.64 minutes a day coiffing themselves. Frankly, this figure seems a tad high, prompting us to believe that some errant Roberts weaseled in and screwed up the curve. Or our Bobs included washing and drying time as well. Still, 5½ minutes is a long car ride from the province of the vainglorious. Bobs strive to achieve a look that isn't a look so much as it is a glance.

BALDING BOBS REVEAL GROOMING REGIMENS

- I spend little time on my hair since my hair seems to be spending little time on me. [96]
- I am splendidly bald. I comb back what is left and go my way. [22]
- I spend just long enough to run a washcloth over it. [114]
- I spend two minutes reminiscing about my hair. [192]
- What hair? [48]

BOBS DESCRIBE THEIR HAIRSTYLES

- Some sort of style. [14]
- Doesn't matter that much. [179]
- I just want to look awake. [108]
- Just shooting for navy grooming standards. [23]
- Just a look that says I'm comfortable with myself. [177]
- I've worn a crew cut for 50 years. Hard to improve. [195]
- Kempt. [24]
- Plain. [202]
- As long as it keeps the top of my head warm, it's okay. [157]
- I don't fuss. [79]
- I hope to look as if I spent only one minute on my hair. [66]
- I don't carry a comb and rely on my fingers to do the trick. [10]
- I like to look as casual as I can. [40]
- My hair does its own thing. [189]

THE LOOKS BOBS STRIVE FOR

- I have never pursued a look. [129]
- The Total Chaos look. [102]
- A Look-Women-Will-Like look. [146]
- The Younger look. [58]
- The Hip Dad look. [69]
- The Short-and-Clean look, opposite of hippies. [84]
- The Rock-and-Roll-Bob look. [141]
- The Not-Scaring-Anyone look. [49]
- The Clint Eastwood look. [161]
- The Yul Brynner look. [204]
- The Pernell Roberts look. [77]
- The Don Johnson look. [68]
- The Less-I-Comb-the-Less-Will-Fall-Out look. [131]
- The Laid-Back-and-Ready-to-Go-on-a-Moment's-Notice look. [158]
- The Perfect Pyramid look. [31]
- The Look-That-Won't-Get-Me-in-Trouble-Since-I'm-in-the-Air-Force look. [193]
- A Mostly Professional look. [123]
- A look of uncaring neatness. [28]
- The Nonoffensive look. [30]

5.64 MINUTES

**AVERAGE TIME BOBS SPEND
ON THEIR
HAIR EACH DAY (PROBABLY
INCLUDES
WASHING AND DRYING TIME)**

truelite Bob tale

IF BOBS DON'T LOOK GOOD...

When is a Bob not a Bob?

When he, um, *it's* a haircut.

More than any other man not named Bob, Vidal Sassoon is inextricably bound to matters bob. Much of his tonsorial career has been given over to bobs. He is said to have brought the bob back at a time when the bob was no more.

The bob flourished first and best in the twenties, of course. Silent-film actress Louise Brooks wore the most famous of bobs. And F. Scott Fitzgerald made Bernice bob her hair in the short story "Bernice Bobs Her Hair." But it wasn't until the early sixties that the old do became the new do. The scissors of Vidal Sassoon rescued the bob from oblivion, where it had been living quietly. Sassoon's bobs stormed onto Carnaby Street, where they pertly flounced atop slinky, sloe-eyed models. From there, the bob spread.

In the years since, the bob has never waned, and much as the sparkle of Mr. Sassoon himself, it has only improved with age. To explore the evolution of bobs, we begged the pixillating British hair-care tycoon to regale us with every bob fact he knew:

What drew you to the bob?

Hair needed to be brought up to date and geometric forms cutting into bone structures will do that.

The bob was the most simple and yet somehow the most difficult to do well. I don't know if this has anything to do with your book, but the whole idea was that every Bob, Dick, Tom, or Harry should want to put his hands through the hair. The whole thing was to make hair sexy. Bob is now part of the universal sex appeal.

This will be news to most Bobs. Describe the bob's best qualities.

The hair is so beautifully swinging. It has body language. It never looks dated.

If bobs don't look good, do you still look good?

Oh no. If a bob doesn't look good, we'll *never* look good.

Who shouldn't wear a bob?

George Bush. Mrs. Bush, also. I love the look she has already. They're wonderful people.

What's the average time a Bob should spend on his hair?

He should get everything done—bathing, hair, with

the best shampoo and conditioner he can find—in twenty minutes to half an hour in the morning, and then not bother about it for the rest of the day. Get on with what's important in life.

Rate the bobs of the twenties?

They all had the *look*, but they didn't have the *cut*. The *cut* was developed in the sixties and a softer version is back in the nineties. It's a wonderful time for hairdressing right now. It's a scissors' delight.

If you could be a famous Bob, which Bob would you be?

It's a shame it wasn't Bob Churchill instead of Winston. Had no hair, poor man, but he had a marvelous mind. He had a bobbed mind.

Since you're British, tell us once and for all: What does "Bob's your uncle" mean?

If you accomplish something you—da da da da—then, "Bob's your uncle." Like, "I've done it." So...Bob's your uncle.

Did you say that after cutting your first bob?

No.

14 THE ROMANTIC BOB

"Women are either right or in a bad mood." —**BOB BOLLING, U.S. District Court clerk**

Women are not exactly Bob-like.

In fact, the opposite of woman is not man so much as it is Bob. While this disparity is by and large a blessing for mankind in general, it is slightly vexing to Bobs. It complicates matters for them. Unlike Bobs, women are wondrously faceted, emotionally textured, and full of surprises. Bobs do not surprise. Nor do they enjoy being surprised. A Bob approaches women—especially in the early going—with the simple forthrightness he looses upon auto mechanics and tax accountants. Bobs classically put their cards on the table and this confounds women who are conditioned to expect subterfuge. To women who crave mystery in men, Bobs require some getting used to. Bobs are served straight-up, whereas women may think they need something with a twist, or a splash, or ultimately, on the rocks.

BOB IN PURSUIT

Bobs are what women want, only women don't always know this. Evenhanded, dependable, and decent, Bobs are probably sometimes mistaken by women for being bland. Therefore, women are often likely to thrash around in a Bob's net, making vain attempts to show Bobs the volatile, mercurial nature of human relations. Bobs find this to be an incredible waste of their time, not to mention that of the woman's. Bobs are loath to engage in love games. Either a Bob calls her or he doesn't call her. That's all. Bobs don't plot. Bobs don't wring their hands and rack their

this way, courtship for Bobs is much like reaching a quota or building a sun deck. It is only when he has completed the project that he must live with the result and that is when a Bob learns a most disconcerting lesson: Women are not finished products. Unlike, say, a wooden fence, women will not just stand there and serve a simple function. They act and react a lot. Their needs go beyond fresh paint. This puzzles Bob.

To Bobs, all women are handfuls. This is the highest of high praise, really. Whether they admit it or not, Bobs need

> *"They're the most wonderful, beautiful things put on this earth and I'm not just saying that because they can completely control and dominate my every breath."*
> —BOB SAGET

central nervous systems and calculate female responses to lunkhead behavior. Bobs would rather play with a lathe.

Still, Bobs are not unromantic. Women force them to discover a world of nuance and subtlety. And Bobs rise to the challenge, learning much in the process (for instance, the finer points of dessert sharing and beholding new and remarkable bathroom rituals). They are good at the chase because they have a goal in mind. In

to be kept guessing; uncertainty of this sort informs their starkly realistic view of existence. Moreover, women color a Bob's life, give it shading and richness and guidance in areas of grooming, dress, and appropriate tipping procedure. Women are the only uncontrollable commodities in a Bob's life, unless we consider Bob's hairline. Unlike baldness, however, women are necessary to Bob, and this, more than anything, is what truly drives him nuts.

101

BOB IN CAPTIVITY

Bobs marry because if they didn't they would only bowl. Bobs marry reflexively. They marry because they must. It is what Bobs are supposed to do.

Once the full flame of passion has dimmed to a steady flicker, what else could there be but marriage? As we have seen, women throw Bobs off balance. Marriage represents every Bob's attempt to rectify matters. For Bobs, marriage makes relationships comprehensible. Bobs withstand the torrents of romance for the sake of marriage and only marriage. It is the clear destination on the road map of love. Like

too much coffee, it is what keeps Bobs driving all night every night, even though they get extremely irritable in the process and wish they could occasionally pull over somewhere to relieve themselves.

Marriage is what Bobs perceive to be a safe harbor, at least until they arrive there. It reminds them of pulling the car into the garage and locking it up for the night: they believe it will be there in the morning. Then they expect it to start up easily and take them only as far as they need to go. Which is to say, Bobs expect from marriage what they expect from life itself: not much, really. Marriage is not an antidote so much as it is a cooling agent.

Still, Bobs fear marriage as much as they desire it. Ideally, partnering up should complement a Bob's slow march along the mortal plain, not impede it. But when Bobs take a wife, they take a risk. They exchange their independence for the opportunity to do many things they would

> *"Women never order dessert, they just eat most of yours."*
> —BOB CLARK, record-company promoter

rather not do or ever consider doing. When Bobs do not understand this at the outset, trouble ensues. To elude any such travail, it is instrumental for Bobs to get an early grasp of Bob's Bookcase Principle.

Bob's Bookcase Principle is as follows: Wives are not bookcases.

Many a Bob has difficulty believing there is a difference between his mate and, say, a bookcase he is building. Well, he

> *"The most important thing to know about women: Do they wear panty hose or garter belts."*
> —BOB MACKIE

knows there are differences. Bookcases don't arouse any mystifying chemical reaction—even though a truly fine piece of wood may well elicit a distinct tingle. But Bobs do sometimes fall into an unhealthy pattern of wishing that their loved ones could be predictable and benign and not

GAL TROUBLE: BOB'S WORDS OF CAUTION

- 1) Most women have a chip on their shoulder about being a woman. 2) Don't marry unless you really want to. [59]
- Learn how to treat them in a loving and caring way without getting hurt yourself. [165]
- They seldom mean what they say, they seldom say what they mean, they often say. [176]
- They are all sluts for something. [146]
- They are tricky. [190]
- They're just like cats. [30]
- Most important to know is that whatever you think you know, they can do just the opposite, just to screw you up. [20]
- If you give them an inch, they'll take a mile. If you think they are lying, they probably are. Most are only after a good time. Don't let them know your true feelings or how much money you're worth. [193]
- There are things they won't tell you. [189]
- They are never wrong. One is always dealing with their emotions. [160]
- Don't trust them. Man, bless his soul, is easy to please. A woman wants everything she sees. [175]
- Don't get involved. [131]

unlike shelving units. With a bookcase, one knows what to expect. Bookcases do not complain of inattention. Bookcases do not wish to dine out regularly. Bookcases never want to go antiquing.

Essentially, Bobs want it on automatic. They want the full fruit of marital bounty, only without having to think too much about it. They are slightly averse to paying close attention to their domestic accord. Instead, they would rather get back to some home-improvement project or a videocassette series on interplanetary tide cycles—the stuff love distracted them from in the first place. It should be no surprise, then, that Bobs are no strangers to divorce.

When Bobs divorce, their innocence is lost and their Bobness is dealt a stunning blow. They learn that what works for them

> *"When lifting, bend your knees. Lift with your legs, not your back!"*
> —BOB PAGANI, radio personality/writer

does not work for others. They learn that women will not behave, in marriage, as complacently as Bobs might have hoped. Bobs then sour on matrimony for a while. During this period, they drink much beer, or potions stiffer, and laugh ruefully when love is mentioned. They snort with great cynicism and frequently say things like, "Hah!" (They are economical even in grousing.) Then they get married again.

Bobs wise up in their second marriages. They have moved, in three separate stages of connubial awareness, from total innocence to total antipathy to total acceptance. When they try again, Bobs avoid

marrying restless women—even though they understand that there will always be *some* restlessness. Women who are successful at being wives of Bobs must be strong, self-assured, self-reliant, and able to amuse themselves when their Bobs are out in the garage. They must also be masterful at calling their Bobs in from the garage when they can stand it no longer.

In the end, Bobs can only be Bobs and women can only be women, and even in marriage, the twain shall never meet, unless it's for breakfast or for dinner and occasionally in front of the television.

> *"Women with great bodies are dangerous."* —BOB DICKINSON,
> restaurant manager

The Quigmans, by Buddy Hickerson, copyright © 1990. Los Angeles Times Syndicate. Reprinted by permission.

WHY BOB FEARS MARRIAGE

"Bob, a single man in his late thirties, is absolutely traumatized at the thought of ever getting married. His greatest concern is that long periods of silence between he and his prospective wife will convince her that she made a terrible mistake, that he's boring and can't maintain a conversation. Bob is so terrified of that possibility that he rarely goes out. When he docs date a woman, he sabotages the relationship early on. When he calls a woman, he prepares all sorts of scripts so that he has something to say, but he still experiences great difficulty maintaining a conversation. Bob cannot accept himself as an okay person without conversational ploys and rehearsals.

"Yet Bob is quite popular amongst his male friends for his amusing sarcastic humor and sense of fun. He is always being invited away on weekend jaunts. His friends know nothing about this problem because he doesn't mind being with another man and having nothing to say. Yet in a continuing self-torture, Bob fantasizes about what it would be like to be married and to have nothing interesting or worthy to say. His obsessive concern is a woman will marry him and therefore throw her life away because she committed herself completely to a nonentity."

—a case study from the self-help text *Why Do I Need You to Like Me in Order to Like Myself?*, by Barry Lubetkin, Ph.D., and Elena Oumano, Ph.D.

HAVING PROBLEMS WITH YOUR FUNNY BONE? SEE BOB.

Bob is a psychologist with some funny problems of his own. Marriage to Suzanne Pleshette is one of them. Peter Bonerz co-stars. THE BOB NEWHART SHOW. NEW SHOW, 9:30PM. WSBC-TV 2 A CBS AFFILIATE

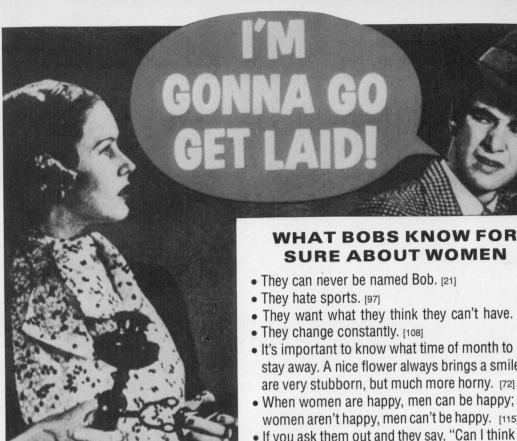

WHAT BOBS KNOW FOR SURE ABOUT WOMEN

- They can never be named Bob. [21]
- They hate sports. [97]
- They want what they think they can't have. [159]
- They change constantly. [108]
- It's important to know what time of month to stay away. A nice flower always brings a smile. They are very stubborn, but much more horny. [72]
- When women are happy, men can be happy; when women aren't happy, men can't be happy. [115]
- If you ask them out and they say, "Can I think about it?" then they really mean "no." [123]
- They never forget anything. [66]
- If you keep company with them, you will spend half your life waiting outside ladies' rooms. [45]
- They take longer. [142]

"All men are stupid. All women are crazy."
—BOB MERLIS, publicist

THE WIFE: BOB'S MARRIAGE MAINTENANCE MANUAL

- Treat them right. [65]
- They like to be told repeatedly how much you love them. They don't like to be kidded about their periods. They are ruthless opponents in court. [161]
- If you don't pay a lot of attention to 'em, they'll go elsewhere. Satisfy the woman before yourself. [23]
- Don't pick a fight unless you really want one. [213]
- When she says, "Tell me what you really think," don't—especially about her hair or clothes. And never send flowers when you're in trouble. [137]
- Treat them with respect and know how to make love to them. [128]
- If their needs are not met, then they are miserable; in turn, it makes your life miserable. If you concentrate on meeting the needs of your mate, your needs will eventually be met too. [40]
- Just remember exactly what you told them last night. [150]
- Know what filling they like best in Fannie Mae candies. [122]
- They just want a little respect. [217]
- Communicate. Take your time. Keep them around as much as possible. [208]
- How to turn them on and how to shut them up. [71]
- Know when to tell her you love her. [18]
- I have only been married 30 years, so I really don't know. [166]

BOB CONFRONTS THE AFFAIR

Scenes From A Bob Marriage: from the film
Bob & Carol & Ted & Alice

Bob's reaction to finding out that Carol's lover is in their bedroom:
"Why didn't you call me? Why didn't you call me and say, 'Bob, I want to have an affair. Can I have an affair?'"
Bob quizzes Carol on the identity of her lover:
"Did I ever shake hands with him?"
Bob trying to be reasonable after Carol explains her lover is in their bedroom:

"I'm not going to do any hitting. I don't believe in wars. I'm not going to hit...Let's be right out in the open about this. Tell him to put his things on and come on down and have a drink with us."
Bob speaking to Carol's Latin lover for the first time:
"Hi, I'm Bob Sanders. Carol's husband. I'm not going to hit you or anything. Nice to know you."

15 THE PATERNAL BOB

"I've always told my kids, be a nice person first and worry about being successful second." —BOB KEESHAN

Bobs make great dads.

They are unobtrusive. They never lord over their litter. Outside of being sentenced to prison time, it's difficult for a child to disappoint a *Pater* Bob. Bobs are less interested in making their young toe the line than they are in having them know where to draw the line. Bobs rule with an invisible hand: Bobness is an exemplary phenomenon no child of Bob's can ignore. Its effect is a subtle, subconscious reminder that a decent life is its own reward. In other words, they don't want their kids to be reprobate scum.

When a Bob names his son Bob, he passes along his Bobness chromosome. Bobness knows no age boundaries. Bobness coalesces early on. For example, the paradigm case of father and son Bob Survey respondents, Big Bob Leary and Little Bob Leary, of Westmont, New Jersey: Little Bob attends grade school. Big Bob is a merchant. We list their responses to the Bob Survey side by side in order to demonstrate the effect of a paternal Bob on his eponymous offspring.

Special Father & Son BoB Survey!

WHY I'M BOB

LITTLE BOB: It's easier to write in a hurry.
BIG BOB: It's simple, direct, easy to remember.

WHAT BEING BOB MEANS

LITTLE BOB: I don't get mixed up with my friend Rob.
BIG BOB: Simple tastes and needs.

MY GREAT WEEKEND

LITTLE BOB: Spending time with my friends, family, and playing more Nintendo.
BIG BOB: Getting away with family and friends. No razors or shoes.

BAD BOBS I'VE KNOWN

LITTLE BOB: None!
BIG BOB: None.

I'M HANDY AT...

LITTLE BOB: Helping my mom clean the dishes.
BIG BOB: Odd jobs around the house and yard.

BEHAVIOR I DISLIKE

LITTLE BOB: When people tease and say things that aren't nice.
BIG BOB: Those who are self-serving, dominant, demeaning.

MY HELL ON EARTH

LITTLE BOB: Going shopping in stores too long.
BIG BOB: Nuclear power plants.

WHO I TRUST AND DISTRUST

LITTLE BOB: I trust my family; I don't trust drunk drivers.
BIG BOB: I trust family and friends; I don't trust strangers and Republicans.

MOST IMPORTANT THING TO KNOW ABOUT WOMEN

LITTLE BOB: To go along with what Mom says.
BIG BOB: When women are happy, men can be happy; when women aren't happy, men can't be happy.

ON MY NIGHTSTAND

LITTLE BOB: A light, pencils, paper, my Walkman, a bear with a Raiders helmet.
BIG BOB: A lamp, telephone, current issue of *National Geographic*, and Grateful Dead tape.

TIME ON HAIR/MY LOOK

LITTLE BOB: I don't spend any time on my hair, my mom does.
BIG BOB: I try to keep my hair neat and out of my face.

COMFORTWEAR

LITTLE BOB: Jeans and T-shirts.
BIG BOB: T-shirts and jeans.

BOYHOOD DREAM

LITTLE BOB: To be a soldier.
BIG BOB: To be an astronaut.

BOB ATTEMPTS PARENTAL GUIDANCE

- Kids, don't make the errors your dad did. [97]
- Go with the flow but earn your own way. Move out of my house by age 21. [109]
- Come to me with any problem and always tell the truth. [165]
- Parents should not teach their kids what to think, but how to think. Respect the power of imagination. [156]
- Name your first son Bob. [9]
- Let them find out for themselves. They'll thank you for it in the long run. [203]
- Leave your world better than we left it to you. [158]
- Kick back from the success treadmill and take a moment out to dig the blues. [140]
- Take care of your father when he's old. [182]
- Save your money so you can support your dad. [87]
- Truly listen to your children instead of just giving them time. [199]
- Watch *The Andy Griffith Show*. Look how Opie turned out. [141]

BOB'S LIST OF DON'TS

- Don't go out with a girl who can beat you at arm wrestling. [159]
- Don't hit women. [94]
- Don't take any crap off anyone. [179]
- Don't be a whiner. (Be a doer.)[23]
- Don't take any shit from anybody. [145]
- Don't waste resources, time, or opportunities. [55]
- Don't ever go into business for yourself. [134]
- Don't be afraid to risk failure. [96]
- Don't allow any person to have complete control of your life. [37]
- Don't get married. [206]
- Never say die. [17]

BOB WE HARDLY KNEW YE

Bobs live and Bobs die.

No doubt, Bob Ryan *would have* completed a Bob Survey. Unfortunately, Bob died, but not without leaving a Bob-like legacy. Bob's children sent a Survey in anyway. Not with what they thought his answers might be, though. Instead, daughter Mary wrote a testimonial to their father. Herewith, we respectfully reprint some of her recollections.

"Our father, Bob Ryan, was the kind of father all the kids on the block would come to talk to, even when they couldn't talk to their own fathers.

"A die-hard Cubs fan, he would (sometimes) sneak us out of school for the games.

"He died of liver failure in his early forties. Over 300 people came to the funeral. Punk kids dressed in their Sunday best to honor him. A conservative neighbor that argued politics with him constantly showed up at the funeral home and saw the sign outside the room that read: 'Robert F. Ryan.' He fetched the funeral-home manager and made him change it. 'His name is Bob,' he said. 'No one ever called him Robert in his life.' "

16 IN BOB WE TRUST

"I distrust fishermen who fish alone."

—BUFFALO BOB SMITH

Bobs never trust anyone who says, "Trust me."

An infinitesimally thin line separates the trustworthy from the suspicious. Bobs can find that line in a snowstorm. Bobs smell fraud the way others smell Danish cheese. Their Bobness serves as a radar system precisely attuned to the integrity of others. This is because Bobs tend to be eminently trustworthy themselves. Bobs are not crafty or sly or misleading. Some Bobs may sell cars for a living, but it is difficult to believe that they are really comfortable doing so. Buying anything from a Bob, however, is a better bet than not buying from a Bob at all. Bobs generally don't have time to screw you over.

Naturally, we place trust in Bobs. What name could be more relentlessly honest? There is no facade in Bob. There is no ruse in Bob. Whereas Roberts must prove themselves first and, for that matter, always. Robs, on the other hand, should never expect to be trusted. And Bobbys may be trustworthy, but also possibly

"Those I don't trust know who they are." —**BOB FELLER**

"I trust the players. I don't trust the owners." —**BOB LITTLE, athletic director**

given to fits of uncontrollable weeping in moments of dire urgency.

Bobs will always Be There.

We rely on Bobs and never think twice about it. You want a Bob to be the catcher in your trapeze act (even though Bobs, as a matter of policy, would take a dim view of circus people). Bobs do the right thing with a vengeance. We relied on Judge Robert "Maximum Bob" Potter to fairly sentence twerpish evangelist cum huckster Jim Bakker. Bakker is currently serving a 45-year prison stint.

We rely on Bob Hope to sing "Silver Bells" with Brooke Shields on his annual TV Christmas specials. He rarely disappoints, at least in that regard.

We willingly leave our offspring in the hands of professional playmates Bob "Captain Kangaroo" Keeshan, Buffalo Bob Smith, Bob (*Sesame Street*) McGrath, and Bob (*Wonderama*) McAllister. These are, after all, grown men.

Bobs are as trusting as they are trustworthy.

On the whole, Bobs are more comfortable trusting. Bobs will give you a chance. Once.

Bobs mostly trust their close friends, parents, children, and current wives. Bobs try never to become too chummy too quickly and are wary of those who do. Bobs don't trust salespeople, carnival workers, weather forecasters, and anyone with two first names. Bobs trust in America, although not necessarily the officials elected to run it.

Now and again, Bobs trust themselves.

But only when they feel as though they've gotten enough background information.

BOBS HAVE NO USE FOR...

- Weather forecasters. [120]
- Young dizzy chicks and salesmen who wear plaid. [66]
- Strangers and Republicans. [115]
- Never trust a real-estate person. [79]
- The IRS. [190]
- Any elected official. [1]
- Backstabbers. [136]
- The service departments of new-car dealerships. [161]
- Sam Donaldson. [19]
- People who like to talk crap: salespeople, politicians, carnival workers, and people with two first names. [179]

- Born-again Christians and telephone solicitors. [151]
- People who try to sell you a Rolex out of their trunk. [146]
- Bobbys. [87]

WHO BOBS TRUST

- Everyone until they do me in. [64]
- Ronald Reagan. [54]
- God. [77]
- Frank Zappa, increasingly. [156]
- My mailman. [82]
- Anyone pragmatic, dependable, and on time. [172]
- Kids under 4 and folks over 70. [166]
- My '64 Nova, truck, and girlfriend. [113]
- Anyone I don't catch lying to me. [10]
- My cat. [106]
- C. Everett Koop. [154]
- Anyone who pays in cash. [170]
- Barbara Bush. [19]
- Anyone who admits they screwed up. [45]
- Anyone who doesn't try too hard to impress me. [158]
- I trust no one. [127]

WHO MAKES BOB LEERY

- Anyone who eats head cheese. [167]
- Anyone who lies—and I eventually find out about it. [32]
- Anyone who says "no strings attached." [137]
- Anyone who doesn't like animals. [183]
- Anyone who tries to become too friendly too fast. [121]
- Anyone who is glib. [163]
- Anyone who is too quiet. [29]
- Anyone named Nick. [61]
- Anyone who takes pen and paper and says, "Let me show you." [195]
- Anyone who slides through life without any effort. [177]
- Anyone who calls himself Mr.-Someone-or-other. [140]
- Anyone who owns more than 15 pairs of shoes. [67]
- Anyone in Penn Station. [95]
- Anyone who says, "Trust me." [91]
- Anyone who says he has my best interests at heart. [83]
- Anyone who seeks too much fame and fortune. [15]
- Anyone, myself included, with a chain saw. [93]

BOB AS GOD

While no one would ever try this with an actual Bob, there is a strange religious order that chose as its deity a figure known as "Bob."

Bobs are unaccustomed to being worshiped. Bobs, as we know them, would find such behavior far too embarrassing and, ultimately, rather difficult to explain to relatives.

"Bob," on the other hand, is a fanciful character, invented by just the sort of overtly eccentric people in whose company no Bob would likely ever be caught dead. "Bob" is one J. R. "Bob" Dobbs, an extremely handsome fellow with a neat haircut and a penchant for pipe smoking. He is the central object of devotion for the Church of the SubGenius, a dizzying cult based in Dallas. The church boasts a mythology that combines aspects of capitalism, communism, nihilism, narcissism, and fundamentalism, all scrambled into an omelet of frenzy, fear, and consumerism. Largely, it is all indecipherable, although further information is available in the church's colorful primer, *The Book of the SubGenius* (Fireside Books).

As for "Bob," it is said that in the early 1950s, he was an industrious young drilling-equipment salesman. While watching late-night TV, he was abruptly transported to an astral plane where he began receiving communications from an alien space god. One thing led to another, as things will, and "Bob" became divine. Soon after, he became known as the High Sales Man of the SubGenius and then "The Man Who Can Sell ANYTHING."

More fun "Bobfacts":

"Bob" is a fornicator; and not just with men and women, but plants too.

"Bob" predicts World Peace in 1998, at 7:00 A.M. on July 5.

"Bob" has a chosen city: Dallas. He'll be there when the Rescue Ships from Planet X arrive.

"Bob" wants you to have Slack. Slack is something taken away from you by the Normals—members of the Conspiracy who would lull you into a slackless sleep. Man and Earth need slack. "Bob" wants you to have slack in order to fight the conspiracy.

"Bob" *is* Slack. "Bob" gives back the Slack stolen by arrogant cashiers and pushy waitresses. Slack is the "Free Car Wash that comes with the fill-up of 'Bob.'"

"Bob" is an imperfect sort who will someday falter in a big way.

"Bob" cusses a lot.

"Bob" really has nothing to say. Which is what he's come to talk with you about.

is a spoiled sports star. Rob is in the movies. Robby's the son of wealthy socialites. Bob's a

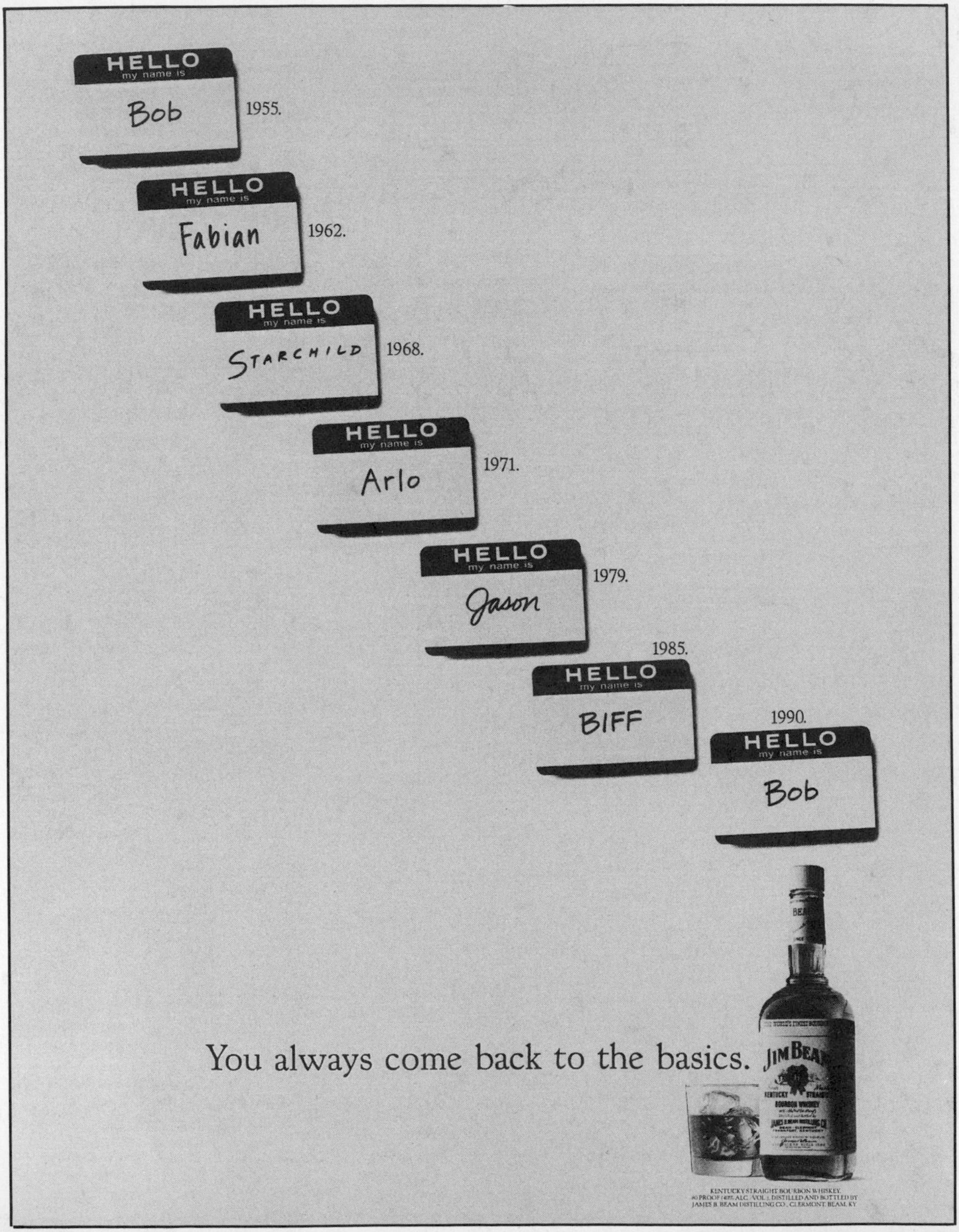

HELLO
my name is
Bob
1955.
HELLO
my name is
Fabian
1962.
HELLO
my name is
STARCHILD
1968.
HELLO
my name is
Arlo
1971.
HELLO
my name is
Jason
1979.
1985.
HELLO
my name is
BIFF
1990.
HELLO
my name is
Bob
You always come back to the basics.
JIM BEAM
KENTUCKY STRAIGHT BOURBON WHISKEY.
80 PROOF (40% ALC./VOL.). DISTILLED AND BOTTLED BY
JAMES B. BEAM DISTILLING CO., CLERMONT, BEAM, KY.

Jim Beam "Back To Basics" Ad: courtesy Jim Beam/American Brands.

BOB IN ADVERTISING

Bobs permeate the commerce of our culture. They populate advertising media in an almost spooky Orwellian fashion: Bobs sell everything. They appear in TV commercials and radio spots (and even print ads when appropriate) as a matter of course. Why? Is it because Bobs are so eminently trustworthy? Is it because those who create advertising have conducted insidious research polls? Or is it all just a cruel joke?

NINE GOOD REASONS WHY BOB IS AMONG THE MOST FREQUENTLY USED NAME IN ADVERTISEMENTS

1. Name always clears legal.
2. Focus groups picked it three-to-one over a dead beetle.
3. Inside slang for a bad spot: according to R. "Bob" Gluckman, copywriter/creator of "ring-around-the-collar."
4. No famous homosexuals named Bob.
5. Most husbands have fantasized about their wives making it with a Bob.
6. Most housewives have fantasized about making it with a Bob.
7. Fun to type.
8. Rounded letters suggest bosoms.
9. Easier to spell than *Caucasian.*
        —Jarl Olson with Bob Barrie, co-creators of Jim Beam's Back To Basics "Hello, My Name Is Bob" ad; Fallon McElligot Agency, Minneapolis

NINE GOOD REASONS WHY SO MANY GUYS IN ADVERTISING ARE NAMED BOB

1. "Bob the adman" more realistic than "Pope Bob."
2. It tested well.
3. Lack of r's and l's a big plus with Japanese clients.
4. Fits easily on golf scorecard.
5. Preferred by Moms, two to one.
6. From a distance, looks like your shirt is monogrammed.
7. Research shows it can be spelled by a whopping 53 percent of brand managers.
8. Contains same number of letters as *new!, wow!,* and *now!*
9. "Hey, we're not married to Bob. If you don't like it, we'll change it."
   —Bob Wolf, CEO of Chiat/Mojo/Day, Los Angeles

The Road to Respect: Chiat/Day/Mojo's 1990 "fantasy" campaign for the Nissan Sentra SE-R conjures a world in which Bob, for the first time ever, receives special treatment

120

17 BAD BOBS (THE RAREST BREED)

"It hurts to find a bad Bob."

—BOB LITTLE, athletic director

There *are* bad Bobs.

The fearsome and vicious albino outlaw in the film *The Life and Times of Judge Roy Bean* was named Bad Bob. The ephemeral evil-spirit BOB (all capital letters) of *Twin Peaks* had a hand in the murder of Laura Palmer. Then there is Bob Shelton, a one-time imperial wizard of the Ku Klux Klan.

Few others come to mind.

Clearly, Bad Bobs are the rarest breed. Any Bob who, on first impression, seems to be less than straightforward is probably just having a bad day. Most Bobs just don't have it in them to be shady.

Even so, we asked hundreds of Bobs if they'd ever met a Bob they didn't like. This question more than any other nudges Bobs, self-effacing or not, toward understanding the meaning of being Bob. More than three-quarters of our respondents have never met a Bob they didn't like.

There are always some rotten apples at the bottom of the barrel. As is Bob's wont, the good Bobs, of course, float to the top.

The rest go back to being Roberts.

121

Special BoB Survey!

BOB PETERSON: SMART-ALECK BOB
Gilder
Billings, Montana

Here is an existentialist Bob, a succinct Bob, one who is both dark and bright, one whose Bobness is artful, brash, and not to be trusted in crowded rooms.

WHY I'M BOB: It was easier to remember.
WHAT BEING BOB MEANS: It means all his clothes fit me.
MY GREAT WEEKEND: Friday, Saturday, Sunday, and Monday.
BAD BOBS I'VE KNOWN: I've never met a Bob I can remember.
I'M HANDY AT...: Putting on my gloves.
BEHAVIOR I DISLIKE: When people sit on me.
MY HELL ON EARTH: Rhonda.
WHO I TRUST AND DISTRUST: Trust: Rhonda. Don't trust: You.
MOST IMPORTANT THINGS TO KNOW ABOUT WOMEN: Breasts and buttocks.
ON MY NIGHTSTAND: Lemon Pledge.
TIME ON HAIR/MY LOOK: Twelve minutes. The Two-Minute look.
COMFORTWEAR: Rubber.
BOYHOOD DREAM: To be Faust.
FREE ADVICE: Take out the garbage and I'll let you live.
FAVORITES:
BOOK: *The Bob Book.*
MOVIE: *Blue Velvet.*
MAGAZINE: *American Handgunner.*

SPORT: Hunting bats in the barn with my tennis racket.
SANDWICH: Liverwurst and onions with mayo.
DRINK: Prune juice.
NEWS ANCHOR: Jack Nicholson.
SMOKE: Leaves burning in the fall.

Special BoB Survey!

ROBERT W. (BOB) SCHEER: ANTI-BOB
Freelance writer
North Vancouver,
British Columbia, Canada

Call him the Anti-Bob. No, him the Anti-Bob. He wants to be Robert. But he can't be Robert, because he is Bob. But he can't be Bob if he wants to be Robert. Call him the Anti-Bob.

WHY I'M BOB: I am trying not to be a Bob anymore. When I meet new people, I try to refer to myself as Robert. The trouble is, sooner or later, I lapse into being Bob. I feel that Robert is much more in control of his own life than Bob is.
WHAT BEING BOB MEANS: As a Bob struggling to be a Robert, I feel that Bob has a potbelly, while

Robert is lean; women regard Bob as a "nice guy," while Robert is a "hunk." Bob wears corduroy, while Robert wears wool.

MY GREAT WEEKEND: Going wine tasting in Mendocino County.

BAD BOBS I'VE KNOWN: I didn't like Bob Ferguson, because I was jealous of him. He was better looking and he had a prettier girlfriend than I did.

I'M HANDY AT...: Making a sauce by deglazing with wine the brown stuff in a frying pan.

BEHAVIOR I DISLIKE: Grammatical errors.

HELL ON EARTH: Having to speak only with people who don't understand that *hopefully* is an adverb.

WHO I TRUST AND DISTRUST: Generally, I trust women and distrust men.

MOST IMPORTANT THING TO KNOW ABOUT WOMEN: What kind of music they really like best.

TIME ON HAIR/MY LOOK: 45 seconds/creative casual.

COMFORTWEAR: Wool sweaters and Levi 501s.

BOYHOOD DREAM: I wanted to write for *Mad* magazine.

FAVORITES:
BOOK: *Tess of the D'Urbervilles*.
TV SHOW: *The Prisoner*.
MAGAZINE: *Bon Appétit*.
CAR: Acura Legend Coupe.
AFTER-SHAVE: Blue Stratos.
SPORT: Formula One motor racing.
DRINK: Malt whisky (Glenfarclas).

SAY IT AIN'T SO! BAD BOBS REMEMBERED

- I had a half-assed friend named Bob. [195]
- There's a Bob in my office who's a power-drunk scumbag. I ignore him at all times. [28]
- Bob was lazy and unmotivated. Bobs *are* motivated and definitely not lazy. [59]
- My cousin Bob. He's a real rocket scientist. [82]
- Only one bad Bob. He drank too much, hit women, and gave all Bobs a bad name. At least today he's in Leavenworth. [211]
- My lawyer, Bob. He's a weasel. [143]
- Sergeant Bob, a real mean drill sergeant I'll never forget. [14]
- I went to high school with one Bob who was a real jerk. He thought he was a great guitar player. Actually, he could hardly play at all. [95]
- Sometimes my dad, Bob. It had to do with me being a teenager at the time. [23]
- My aunt's husband, Bob. He was a self-centered, self-important jerk who rubbed just about everyone, including his wife, the wrong way. She divorced him. He's dead now. [112]
- Bob Dennis is a disgrace to the name. Don't let him in the book. [130]
- Bob Smith used to beat me up in grade school. He was big and fat. [148]
- Bobcat Goldthwait. Can anyone understand this comedian? [102]

"When I meet a Bob, my first inclination is to like the guy."
—BOB CLARK, public administrator

18 WHAT BOBS KNOW FOR SURE

"Be patient with people, realize that something will probably go wrong, and don't loan out your tools."

—BOB KENTON BROWN, salesman

"Your name and your word are it."

—BOB McKINZIE, truck driver

What Bobs know they keep to themselves.

Unless they are asked.

Because Bobs know what's what and how it specifically applies to them and only them, they are reluctant oracles. Bobs don't go around telling others how to live their lives, even though if there were room for improvement, Bobs would certainly be aware of it. Bobs have figured out life. Bobs know what works. By taking a minimalist approach, Bobs know all they need to know, and it isn't really any of our business. Why, for example, did Bob cross the road? Because he had his reasons. That's all.

The Big Questions aren't all that important to Bobs. Bobs do not want to know the Meaning of Life so much as they want to know the meaning of "Louie Louie" by the Kingsmen. Bobs do not want to think about their role in the cosmos. They just want to get through the week. If there were any Big Answers to be found, Bobs assume someone would have said something by now.

After a lifetime of searching, Bob stumbles across the meaning of life quite accidentally.

Bobs live by an ethos. They live by a code of practical values, time-honored principles, and excessive perspiration. Because Bobs must someday urge good sense upon their progeny, they keep at the ready the most basic and eloquent guidelines of how not to screw up. The wisdom of Bobs is at once simple and profound. When we asked Bobs to impart their philosophies in the Bob Survey, we expected solid, tangible advice. That is, we expected the expected.

BOB'S PHILOSOPHY

- Life is for living. Enjoy every minute. [148]
- Be yourself. [111]
- Be a nice guy. [212]
- Be happy. Give lots of love and be kind. [128]
- It's not the destination, it's the journey. [16]
- Don't worry. It doesn't do any good. [218]
- Don't stress out. [29]
- A lousy day fishing is better than the best day working. [70]

BOB'S RULES OF ORDER

- Watch your ass. [132]
- Seek to avoid unhappiness instead of pursuing happiness. [187]
- Believe in yourself. Eat a variety of foods. But all in moderation. [142]
- Be honest but don't turn your back. [163]
- Polonius's advice in *Hamlet*: "To thine own self be true." [84]
- Absorb whatever wisdom you can find, without becoming a devotee of anyone, no matter how brilliant or charismatic. Live simply but don't be a fanatic about it. Splash about in water whenever possible. [185]
- Be kind with thoughts and money. Remember, not everyone has a trust fund. [126]
- Always tell the truth even when you don't want to. [22]
- Be able to look a total stranger in the eye and spout with a friendly air, "Do you have that ten dollars you owe me?" [anon]
- Live a life that makes you like yourself. [5]

- You have to provide and take care of yourself. [198]
- Ask a lot of questions. [46]
- Have strong moral and hygienic values. [155]

SURVEY STATS: BOBS' FAVORITES

BOBS' FAVORITE BOOK
Bible; Stephen King novels

BOBS' FAVORITE AFTER-SHAVE
None

BOBS' FAVORITE SPORT
Football

BOBS' FAVORITE SANDWICH
Ham and cheese

BOBS' FAVORITE DRINK
Beer

BOBS' FAVORITE SMOKE
None

BOBS' FAVORITE NEWS ANCHOR
Peter Jennings

BOBS' FAVORITE MOVIE
It's a Wonderful Life

BOBS' FAVORITE TV SHOW
Cheers

BOBS' FAVORITE MAGAZINE
Sports Illustrated

BOBS' FAVORITE BREAKFAST CEREAL
Raisin Bran

BOBS' FAVORITE CAR
Corvette

WHAT BOBS KNOW FOR SURE

- Nothing is new. [20]
- History as written does not include what happened. [89]
- Life is not fair, you make your own luck, and education is the key to success. [161]
- College is the greatest time that you'll ever have in your life. [82]
- Money is made to spend on people's needs and women are made to love. [36]
- Integrity and a good reputation are important. [215]
- Peace, love, sports. [53]
- A man is as good as his word. There is no shame in walking away from something that doesn't feel right. [22]
- What goes around comes around. [69]
- Anything is possible. [55]
- Life is hard but can be fun if the rules are ignored. [18]
- Life is not a dress rehearsal. [1]
- Discipline is the essence of life. [173]
- Life is an onion. You peel away one layer at a time, and sometimes you weep. [10]

BOB'S BOTTOM LINE

- Do the right thing. [83]
- Be good in sports and you'll be a millionaire. [71]
- If you don't know, say so. It's easy to learn. Thirty percent is great if you gave it your best shot. But 70 percent is unacceptable if you're capable of 90 percent. [169]
- No matter what, don't give up your goals. [73]
- Give it your best shot. [210]
- Work hard and be on time. [195]
- Strive to achieve…compassionately. [77]
- A good loser is *always* a loser. [60]
- Do your best and don't look back. [19]

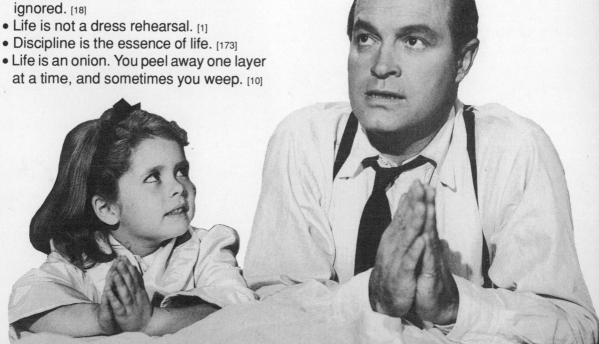

THE BOB WHO STUFFED
EUROPE WITH PIZZA

Bob Payton knew this for sure: The English were bad at pizza.

Few things could be as unsettling to an American Bob in London. And Bob Payton was just such a Bob. In 1977, he was an ad man in exile, having been transferred from J. Walter Thompson's Chicago headquarters to the London branch office. Languishing in a kingdom known for its warm beer and aversion to ice cubes, Payton was especially bedeviled by the dearth of solid, no-fuss American cuisine. "My version of hell on earth," he told *The Bob Book*, "is the thought of not being able to have a decent pizza or good rare cheeseburger when I want it." In fact, when on one night that year it took thirteen wispy English pizzas to sate Payton and a few comrades, this Bob could stand no more.

He raised dough and promptly opened The Chicago Pizza Pie Factory, an authentic American pizzeria serving hefty deep-dish Chicago-style pizzas in St. James's, just down the road from Buckingham Palace. He plastered the walls with hometown sports memorabilia and piped in Chicago radio tapes. He made $1.3 million the first year. Now, besides the London flagship, Bob has opened Pizza Pie Factories in Barcelona, Paris, Dublin, Bonn, Tel Aviv, and Madrid, just in case he needs decent pizza when roaming Europe.

In this way, Bob made Bobness a capitalist tool.

"I couldn't eat pizza every day of the week," says Bob, who eventually decided he was hankering for some decent ribs (The Chicago Rib Shack: London), T-bone steak (The Chicago Meatpackers: London, Paris, and Glasgow), and hot dogs and chili (Henry J. Bean's: London, Aberdeen, Manchester, Barcelona, and Brussels). His Bob empire, the so-called My Kinda Town, Ltd. restaurants, all of which serve regular Chicago beer (cold), draws an annual volume, at last count, of roughly $40 million. Bob even opened a grand country house hotel called Stapleford Park in Leicestershire, where Bob tends to run around the lobby prodding English guests, "Hey! What's everybody so quiet for? You've got to make some noise!" Bob, because he's a Bob, can often be seen carrying luggage up to rooms.

"My success," says Bob, "has a lot to do with being single-minded." As evidence, Payton also publishes a quintessentially Bob-friendly handbook called, *The Chicagoan's Guide to London*, in which, among other vital tips, he discourses on the vagaries of ordering beer in Great Britain: "If you want what we [Americans] call beer, ask for a *lager*," Bob writes. "If you want to drink the local brew, order a pint of *bitter*, not bitters. Say to the bartender, 'Let me have a pint of *best*.'" Bob also warns that, because most pubs are closed in daytime, "It is still reasonably difficult to get a nice cold beer on a nice warm English afternoon." So, basically, he seems to be saying, Let the Bob beware.

PART THREE:

THE CELEBRATED BOB

It is the rare Bob who actually seeks notoriety, who truly craves renown. But now and again, if only because Bobs are hardworking guys, they can't avoid recognition. When it happens, they're characteristically unpretentious about it. Which seems to explain why so many famous Bobs didn't mind playing along with the Bob Survey.

19 FAMOUS BOBS TAKE THE BOB SURVEY

BOB BARKER, game-show host/animal rights activist, Los Angeles, California

Bob Barker is the perennial host of *The Price Is Right*.

WHY I'M BOB: I am part Sioux and grew up on the Rosebud Reservation in South Dakota; my name is Robert William and I was called "Bill." But the Indian Department kept bugging my mother about whether Robert was in school, so she had to admit that I am "Bob."

WHAT BEING BOB MEANS: It means that the government stopped bugging my mother.

MY GREAT WEEKEND: Lying in the sun doing absolutely nothing.

BAD BOBS I'VE KNOWN: They were as offensive as the Toms, Freds, Carls, and Luthers—etc.

I'M HANDY AT...: Changing light bulbs. I can do it by myself.

BEHAVIOR I DISLIKE: Violent.

MY HELL ON EARTH: Watching *The Gong Show*.

WHO I TRUST AND DISTRUST: I trust Mother. I don't trust the others.

MOST IMPORTANT THING TO KNOW ABOUT WOMEN: Which is which.

ON MY NIGHTSTAND: My cat.

TIME ON MY HAIR/MY LOOK: Lots of time/I want to be sure that every hair is doing its job.

COMFORTWEAR: My wedding ring.

BOYHOOD DREAM: I wanted to pitch for the St. Louis Cardinals. Their manager, Whitey Herzog, read about this dream in an interview and signed me to a contract for a dollar a year so long as I *don't* pitch.

FREE ADVICE: Having children is hereditary. If your parents don't have children, you probably won't have children either.

FAVORITES:

BOOK: Driver's Manual.

MOVIE: Whatever is on TV when I have time to watch.

TV SHOW: *The Price Is Right*.

MAGAZINE: *Discounts for the Elderly*.

CEREAL: A donut.

CAR: Kaiser.

AFTER-SHAVE: Mercurochrome.

SPORT: "Bob" sledding.

SANDWICH: Peanut butter and avocado.

DRINK: Please.

NEWS ANCHOR: Phyllis George.

SMOKE: No thanks.

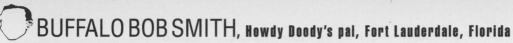

BUFFALO BOB SMITH, Howdy Doody's pal, Fort Lauderdale, Florida

Buffalo Bob Smith—onetime resident of Buffalo, New York—has been pulling Howdy Doody's strings since 1947.

WHY I'M BOB: Simply because I preferred it. It seemed to suit me better.

WHAT BEING BOB MEANS: It's a good boy's name. Better than Clarence, Oscar, or Elmer.

MY GREAT WEEKEND: Playing golf or fishing on a Saturday. Going to church on Sunday. Being at home watching sports on TV with my wife. Cooking out on Saturdays for special friends.

BAD BOBS I'VE KNOWN: I've met several Bobs I didn't particularly like. Also Johns, Jacks, Bills, Charlies, and Martins. How could one like or dislike a person just because of his first name?

I'M HANDY AT...: Playing piano—if you mean something to do with your hands. Or cooking or repairing anything simple.

BEHAVIOR I DISLIKE: Overdrinking and becoming loud and obnoxious. Smoking, including cigarettes, cigars, and pipes. Especially when I'm tired.

MY HELL ON EARTH: Having a miserable cold and being confined in a room with people who are overdrinking, loud and obnoxious, and smoking cigarettes, pipes, or cigars. Especially when I'm tired or have played golf badly.

WHO I TRUST AND DISTRUST: I trust in God, my wife, and my family and several business associates and friends. I don't trust golfers with phony handicaps or fishermen who fish alone and catch record fish without a camera for proof.

MOST IMPORTANT THINGS TO KNOW ABOUT WOMEN: Their likes and dislikes.

ON MY NIGHTSTAND: A lamp, clock radio, telephone, flashlight, and fresh glass of water.

TIME ON MY HAIR/MY LOOK: Two to three minutes; washing it daily—towel drying, combing. Trying to achieve the same look I've had for the past 50 years.

COMFORTWEAR: Casual golf or fishing clothes. Because I do both.

BOYHOOD DREAM: To be a musician and singer.

FREE ADVICE: Work hard at what you enjoy doing. Be loyal and honest. Be true and faithful to your Lord.

FAVORITES:

BOOK: Bank book.

MOVIE: *The Godfather* and *The Sting*.

TV SHOW: *Howdy Doody* and *I Love Lucy*.

MAGAZINE: *New Yorker*.

CEREAL: Kelloggs Frosted Flakes.

CAR: BMW 750-IL, by far.

AFTER-SHAVE: Mennen Skin Bracer.

SPORT: Golf, baseball.

SANDWICH: Brisket of beef on kummelweck roll.

DRINK: Absolut vodka (citron).

NEWS ANCHOR: Ted Koppel: He looks more like Howdy Doody than the others.

SMOKE: I thought the only people who smoked couldn't read.

BOB COSTAS, sportscaster, St. Louis, Missouri

Bob Costas is the host of NBC-TV's *Later... With Bob Costas*, and does network play-by-play.

WHY I'M BOB: Robert's too formal for a sportscaster and I look young enough without being Bobby or Rob.

WHAT BEING BOB MEANS: It means I'm not George, Harry, or Louie.

BAD BOBS I'VE KNOWN: From a distance, I wasn't so thrilled with H. R. "Bob" Haldeman.

BEHAVIOR I DISLIKE: People asking me impertinent questions about myself.
COMFORTWEAR: An evening gown, stiletto heels, and a garter belt.
BOYHOOD DREAM: To be a sportscaster, specifically a baseball announcer.
FAVORITES:
BOOK: *Charlotte's Web.*
MOVIE: *King Kong.*
TV SHOW: *The Honeymooners.*
MAGAZINE: *Boys Life* and *Highlights.*
CEREAL: Spoon-sized Shredded Wheat.
CAR: Edsel.
AFTER-SHAVE: Old Spice—like a real man.
SPORT: Baseball—like a real American.
SANDWICH: Peanut butter and jelly on Wonder Bread.
DRINK: A vanilla egg cream at a NY deli.
NEWS ANCHOR: Albert Brooks in *Broadcast News.*
SMOKE: Unfiltered Lucky Strikes.

BOB CUMMINGS, actor, Sherman Oaks, California

The late Bob Cummings had three network-TV series, one of which was *Love That Bob*, a phrase for which all Bobs remain in his debt.
WHY I'M BOB: Because anyone named Robert is automatically known as Bob.
WHAT BEING BOB MEANS: That almost everyone treats you as if they'd known you for years—even if it's the first time they meet you.
MY GREAT WEEKEND: Spending it with my wonderful new wife, Janie.
BAD BOBS I'VE KNOWN: None.
I'M HANDY AT...: Acting and flying airplanes.
BEHAVIOR I DISLIKE: That of an IRS officer during an audit.
MY HELL ON EARTH: Opening night when you're starring in a Broadway show.
WHO I TRUST AND DISTRUST: I trust most schoolteachers. I don't trust politicians.
MOST IMPORTANT THING TO KNOW ABOUT WOMEN: Their astrological birth sign.
ON MY NIGHTSTAND: Almost everything I own.
TIME ON MY HAIR/MY LOOK: About two minutes/The Bob Cummings Crew-cut look.
COMFORTWEAR: Long wool underwear.
BOYHOOD DREAM: To be an aeronautical engineer.
FREE ADVICE: You can accomplish anything in the universe by <u>acting</u>—acting with all your heart—as if it's already accomplished!
FAVORITES:
BOOK: The *International Almanac.*
MOVIE: *King's Row.*
TV SHOW: *The Golden Girls.*
MAGAZINE: *National Geographic.*
CEREAL: Skinner's Bran Flakes.
CAR: Chevrolet.
AFTER-SHAVE: Gray Flannel.
SPORT: Volleyball.
SANDWICH: Club.
DRINK: Papaya juice.
NEWS ANCHOR: Jerry Dunphy.

BOB DENVER, actor, Las Vegas, Nevada

Bob Denver is Gilligan. Bob Denver will always be Gilligan. Bob Denver is also Maynard G. Krebs, but mostly he's Gilligan.
WHY I'M BOB: For the esoteric value.
WHAT BEING BOB MEANS: Doesn't <u>mean</u> anything!

MY GREAT WEEKEND: Sailing a 59′ 6″ schooner with my wife and child to Moorea.
BAD BOBS I'VE KNOWN: Some, but then I've also met Daves and Bills I didn't like.
I'M HANDY AT...: My wife says I'm handy at everything.
BEHAVIOR I DISLIKE: That of loud, boring, self-centered, egotistical people.
MY HELL ON EARTH: Sitting beside the above at a formal dinner party with too many utensils.
WHO I TRUST: My wife, Dreama.
MOST IMPORTANT THINGS TO KNOW ABOUT WOMEN: I don't know—I really don't know.
ON MY NIGHTSTAND: I don't have a nightstand.
TIME ON MY HAIR: Five minutes.
COMFORTWEAR: Something with memories.
BOYHOOD DREAM: To be a pilot.
FREE ADVICE: Do not impose your own philosophies on your children.
FAVORITES:
BOOK: *Horton Hatches the Egg.*
MOVIE: *Mr. Hulot's Holiday.*

TV SHOW: *Life Goes On.*
MAGAZINE: *Science.*
CEREAL: S.W. Grahams.
CAR: 1966 XKE Roadster Convertible.
AFTER-SHAVE: None.
SPORT: Football, golf.
SANDWICH: BLT on T.
DRINK: Coffee.
NEWS ANCHOR: Tom Brokaw.
SMOKE: Santa Fe on a cold October morning.

 BOB DOLE, Republican senator from Kansas, Washington, D.C.

Senate Republican Leader Bob Dole has twice sought his party's presidential nomination.

WHY I'M BOB: I wanted to be the first Bob president.
MY GREAT WEEKEND: A weekend with Elizabeth and no phones, no votes, no travel, good sun, Sunday brunch, the Sunday papers, and my exercise treadmill.
I'M HANDY AT...: Giving orders.
MY HELL ON EARTH: An all-night Senate session.
ON MY NIGHTSTAND: Alarm clock, flashlight.
BOYHOOD DREAM: To be a doctor.
FAVORITES:
BOOK: *Eisenhower—the President,* by Stephen E. Ambrose.
MOVIE: *Gone With the Wind.*
TV SHOW: *Murder, She Wrote.*
CEREAL: Oatmeal.
CAR: American.
SONG: Anything by Glenn Miller or Dionne Warwick.
SPORT: Basketball.
SANDWICH: Hamburger.
DRINK: Coffee.
SMOKE: No thanks.

 BOB DYLAN, musician, Malibu, California

Bob Dylan was born Robert Allan Zimmerman in Duluth, Minnesota. When he decided to sing for a living, he jettisoned the Zimmerman, but kept the Bob. Hmmm.

He is unlike many Bobs in that he is enigmatic. However, in the truest spirit of Bob, he is at least *dependably* enigmatic. As George Harrison succinctly put it: "Bob is still out there, and whether you like him or not, he's still Bob."

In his dependably enigmatic way, Bob Dylan chose to answer only one question in the Bob Survey:

FREE ADVICE: Don't do to someone something you wouldn't want them to do to you.

BOB EINSTEIN, actor: "Super Dave Osborne," Los Angeles, California

For professional reasons, Bob Einstein is known to thrill-seeking fans of his Showtime series as Super Dave Osborne. He was formerly Officer Judy on the *Smothers Brothers Comedy Hour.* Nevertheless, he is a Bob.

WHY I'M BOB: Because I just like the sound. The reason I use the name Super Dave Osborne is because if I had used my real name I would have been Super Bob Einstein, and if I had gotten hurt at a stunt the first thing the paramedics would have asked is what's your name. If I answered "Bob Einstein..." they would have asked, "Any relation?" In that split second I could have bled to death.

WHAT BEING BOB MEANS: It means I'm not Phil.

MY GREAT WEEKEND: Two perfect days in Maui. Golf. Driving in a convertible. Sailing. Great food. Surrounded by loved ones. Beautiful sunrises, sunsets, Son of Sam—anything with sun in it. My spirits are much better in beautiful weather.

BAD BOBS I'VE KNOWN: Maybe it's just harder to dislike a Bob. We're very lucky that some of the terrible people in this world have not been named Bob. Can you a imagine a Bob Hitler or Bob Manson?

I'M HANDY AT...: Turning down people for books like this.

BEHAVIOR I DISLIKE: Dishonesty. Cheapness. Rudeness. And I'm not terribly fond of people who shoot other people when they drive by.

MY HELL ON EARTH: Finding out you were adopted and your given name was really Bob Gabor.

WHO I TRUST AND DISTRUST: I trust people who are genuinely kind, giving, and spiritual, who put the trials and tribulations of others before their own. In other words, I don't trust anyone. Or anyone without a sense of humor; or anyone who says "trust me."

MOST IMPORTANT THINGS TO KNOW ABOUT WOMEN: Are they honest? Are they truly kind? Are they sensitive and loving and caring? And, most important, have they ever been on *Geraldo*?

ON MY NIGHTSTAND: A copy of your letter asking me to fill out this goddamned questionnaire.

TIME ON MY HAIR/MY LOOK: I don't spend that much time/the Don King look.

COMFORTWEAR: Casual clothes.

BOYHOOD DREAM: Just to be happy and healthy.

FREE ADVICE: Treat other people with respect and you'll get it back. Be honest, humble, and try to see everything in life through humorous eyes.

FAVORITES:
BOOK: *Exodus.*
MOVIE: *The Godfather.*
TV SHOW: *Super Dave Osborne.*
MAGAZINE: *Playboy.*
CEREAL: Goat Bran.

CAR: Jeep Grand Wagoneer.
SONG: "The Name Game" by Shirley Ellis.
AFTER-SHAVE: I don't need any.
SPORT: Basketball or golf.
SANDWICH: Turkey, bacon, lettuce, tomato, mayo on sourdough.
DRINK: Margarita or vodka and cranberry juice.
NEWS ANCHOR: Peter Jennings.
SMOKE: Never in my life.

 # BOB ELLIOT, comedian/actor/writer, New York City

Bob Elliot was the Bob in the legendary comedy partnership Bob and Ray.

WHY I'M BOB: It was the name I was called most often growing up and in school, and the name I used on the air in my first radio announcing job. Never used any other form of Robert.

WHAT BEING BOB MEANS: That I've always gotten top billing over Ray, although he was much the funnier one. But when you come to think of it, Andy was funnier than Amos; Allen funnier than Burns; Abner funnier than Lum; Costello funnier than Abbott; Lewis funnier than Martin.

Before *Bob and Ray*, I did a disc jockey show called *Back Bay Matinee*. We teamed up for a pre-baseball broadcast called *Baseball Matinee*, and when the season ended, the station (wanting to retain the "matinee" idea) called our show *Matinee with Bob and Ray*. Otherwise it would have had to have been "Mantinob with Ray and Bob."

MY GREAT WEEKEND: Enjoying New York City as the adopted hometown it is; the *Times* Sunday Crossword and brunch at Rusty's.

BAD BOBS I'VE KNOWN: Just one. Bob Andre, a program director I once knew who had no sense of humor.

I'M HANDY AT...: Painting—mostly watercolors—and woodworking; building. With the exception of plumbing and wiring, I once built an entire home (which still stands) and used only a handsaw. (I was afraid of the newly introduced power models!)

BEHAVIOR I DISLIKE: Exuding a superior attitude.

WHO I TRUST AND DISTRUST: My wife—implicitly. I trust her views in all things, have great respect for her opinions, and marvel at her ability to get to the bottom of things. As a general rule I don't trust lawyers. And I'm not too thrilled by judges, either.

ON MY NIGHTSTAND: Clock radio on WNEW-AM, half roll of Rolaids, opened package of Fisherman's Friends cough lozenges, Afrin Nasal Spray, handkerchief, lamp, flashlight, notepad, pen.

TIME ON MY HAIR: Thirty seconds. But the job takes less time week by week!

COMFORTWEAR: Jeans, L. L. Bean's Ranger Oxfords, turtlenecks. Navy blazers and gray slacks, loafers. Brooks shirts, suits.

BOYHOOD DREAM: From the time I knew what radio was I wanted to be part of it. Had my eyes on an announcer's job until I got it in 1941. With three years out for the army I returned to the job in 1946 and one thing led to another.

FREE ADVICE: We have three daughters and two sons; eleven grandchildren. My youngest boy, Chris, is the only one in this business (on the *Letterman Show*) although most of the others tried a couple of seasons in summer stock, ending

up in more prosaic life-styles. I left it to them to absorb whatever of my philosophy came through.

FAVORITES:
BOOK: *Time and Again* by Jack Finney.
MOVIE: Any by Woody Allen.
TV SHOW: Miniseries, news, *48 Hours, 60 Minutes*.
MAGAZINE: *Down East.*
CEREAL: Latest one out: currently Heartwise.
CAR: My 1959 Ford Galaxie.
SONG: "Moonlight Serenade" by Glenn Miller.
AFTER-SHAVE: Aramis.
SPORT: Baseball.
SANDWICH: Monte Christo.
DRINK: White wine.
NEWS ANCHOR: Dan Rather.

 **BOB EUBANKS, entrepreneur/game-show host, Los Angeles, California**

Bob Eubanks is best known for hosting the *Newlywed Game* as well as the *New Newlywed Game*. On both, he was eternally inquisitive about the contestants' "whoopie-making" skills. But he had to be. It was his job.

WHY I'M BOB: Because you can spell it backward and still get it right. And it's so rhythmic: Bob. Bob. Bob. Only the IRS calls me Robert. I had an aunt who called me Bobby Lee and I wouldn't speak to her for 23 years.

WHAT BEING BOB MEANS: It means you're over 50. Do you know many Bobs under 50? Bob is certainly not a Yuppie name. I don't even think this book can bring it back, although I'm hopeful.

MY GREAT WEEKEND: To play golf one day and to go to the rodeo the next day. My youngest son and I rope together. And since I'm above 50, good-looking horses are the only things I look at.

BAD BOBS I'VE KNOWN: There have been a couple. They were both big braggarts.

I'M HANDY AT...: I am so unmechanical and so unhandy that I cannot even defrost a refrigerator. One time I worked at Lockheed for three days, and at the end of the third day, I had to turn in the only toolbox I ever owned. They asked me not to come back.

BEHAVIOR I DISLIKE: That of loud people, people who chew with their mouths open, or people who yell at you from across the room. And braggarts.

MY HELL ON EARTH: When you're in third place out of three networks in the ratings.

WHO I TRUST AND DISTRUST: I trust almost anybody until they screw me. I trust anybody whose name is not Michael Moore.

MOST IMPORTANT THINGS TO KNOW ABOUT WOMEN: They rule the earth. When we're born, they put a nipple in our mouth, when we're five years old, they take us by the hand, and then when we're twenty, they grab us between the legs and lead us around for the rest of our lives.

ON MY NIGHTSTAND: Two alarm clocks and a candle. I don't want to oversleep and when the lights go out I want to be able to see when I get up to go to the bathroom.

TIME ON HAIR/MY LOOK: As I get older I spend less time, because I have less hair to spend time on. Fullness.

COMFORTWEAR: I'm strictly a Wrangler jeans, cowboy boots, and sweatshirts kind of guy.

BOYHOOD DREAM: First to be a pilot, then to be a disc jockey.
FREE ADVICE: Don't have more than one child. Just kidding. Don't give kids too much and at the age of eighteen make them your friend.
FAVORITES:
BOOK: *To Kill a Mockingbird.*
MOVIE: *One Flew Over the Cuckoo's Nest.*
TV SHOW: I love *The Wonder Years* because it reminds me of when my kids were growing up.
MAGAZINE: *Golf Digest.*
CEREAL: Frosted Flakes was my favorite, now I eat NutriGrain.
CAR: Porsche 900? 911? 914?
SONG: "Always on My Mind," Willie Nelson.
AFTER-SHAVE: Calvin Klein Obsession.
SPORT: Golf, rodeo.
SANDWICH: Peanut butter and jelly. That's Bob, huh?
DRINK: Iced decaf.
NEWS ANCHOR: Peter Jennings, even though he says "with-ooot."

BOB EVANS, founder of Bob Evans Farms, Gallipolis, Ohio

Bob Evans believes in honest pork sausages, which is a good thing when one is left to consider what may be inside of a dishonest pork sausage. He owns five meat-packing plants and over 226 family restaurants.

WHY I'M BOB: It's a good family name. I'm named after both of my grandfathers: Bob Evans and Bob Lewis.
BAD BOBS I'VE KNOWN: He had a bad personality.
MY GREAT WEEKEND: Spending time out of doors—horseback riding or walking.
I'M HANDY AT...: Keeping from eating too much.
BEHAVIOR I DISLIKE: Smoking or telling me how rich I am.
MY HELL ON EARTH: Living in the inner city.
WHO I TRUST AND DISTRUST: I trust farmers. I don't trust lawyers.
MOST IMPORTANT THINGS TO KNOW ABOUT WOMEN: Some are great; however, they rule the world.
ON MY NIGHTSTAND: A phone.
TIME ON MY HAIR/MY LOOK: Five minutes/clean.
COMFORTWEAR: Old clothes.
BOYHOOD DREAM: To be a conservation expert.
FREE ADVICE: The harder you work, the better your luck is.
FAVORITES:
BOOK: *How to Win Friends and Influence People.*
MOVIE: *Gone With the Wind.*
TV SHOW: *Sanford and Son.*
MAGAZINE: *Fortune.*
CEREAL: Grape Nuts.
CAR: Lincoln Continental.
SONG: "How Great Thou Art."
AFTER-SHAVE: None.
SPORT: Baseball.
SANDWICH: Country ham.
DRINK: Coffee.
NEWS ANCHOR: Jane Pauley.
SMOKE: None.

BOB FELLER, Cleveland Indians pitcher, 1936–56, Gates Mills, Ohio

For many years Bob Feller was the fastest Bob in baseball. He was inducted into the

Hall of Fame in 1962 and recently penned his autobiography, *Now Pitching... Bob Feller*.

WHY I'M BOB: My father called me Son, my mother called me Robert. Everyone else called me Bob and a few Bobby. I really never tried to steer my name in any specific direction.

WHAT BEING BOB MEANS: To have been an athlete—a good one—and to have achieved many goals I set for myself as a young boy. Now, to be a husband and a friend to—I hope—many people.

MY GREAT WEEKEND: To be at home having hamburgers or hot dogs outdoors or grilling a steak and eating on our deck with my wife Anne or a few friends. On the road or away from home it could be a lot of things such as visiting museums or going to a tractor fair.

BAD BOBS I'VE KNOWN: There may be some but not anyone I remember.

I'M HANDY AT...: Working with machinery.

BEHAVIOR I DISLIKE: Loud and not considerate of others.

MY HELL ON EARTH: It's not "hell on earth," but listening to a speaker who goes far beyond his or her allotted time.

WHO I TRUST AND DISTRUST: I trust my wife and many of my close friends. Those I don't trust know who they are.

MOST IMPORTANT THINGS TO KNOW ABOUT WOMEN: They do a good job as volunteers and work hard for causes they believe in.

ON MY NIGHTSTAND: A clock, flashlight, telephone, several pictures, and a stuffed bear.

TIME ON MY HAIR/MY LOOK: About 30 seconds/neat.

COMFORTWEAR: Cotton work shirts and work pants—around our farm.

BOYHOOD DREAM: To be a baseball player.

FREE ADVICE: Work hard, plan, prepare, save, and be honest.

FAVORITES:

BOOK: *Rickenbacker, An Autobiography*.

MOVIE: *The Kid from Cleveland*.

TV SHOW: I don't watch much TV.

MAGAZINE: *National Geographic*.

CEREAL: Product 19. The Indians retired my number 19. Is this loyal or what?

CAR: Ford.

SONG: Our National Anthem. I heard it before every ballgame.

AFTER-SHAVE: Witch hazel.

SPORT: Baseball.

SANDWICH: Peanut butter.

DRINK: Milk.

NEWS ANCHOR: Peter Jennings.

SMOKE: Never smoked.

 BOB GOEN, game-show host, Beverly Hills, California

Bob Goen grew up to be the game-show host (daytime *Wheel of Fortune*) he always wanted to be. He knows Vanna White personally.

WHY I'M BOB: It seemed like the perfect compromise between formality (Robert) and frivolity (Bobby). Plus, it's easier to spell.

WHAT BEING BOB MEANS: It means you have to be either a game-show host or a gas station attendant...both of which I have been.

BAD BOBS I'VE KNOWN: He worked with me at the gas station. We constantly argued over the pros and cons of having windows on the sides of your van, and he told me how cool his goatee was when he let it grow out. Also, Shish-kabob.

I'M HANDY AT...: Anything around the house with large power tools.

BEHAVIOR I DISLIKE: Arrogance. I'd rather hear through the grapevine that you have eight-percent body fat than have you tell me yourself.

MY HELL ON EARTH: Having a gym locker next to a guy with eight-percent body fat.

WHO I TRUST AND DISTRUST: I trust anyone with two large dogs, especially golden retrievers. I don't trust anyone who uses the word *indeed*.

MOST IMPORTANT THINGS TO KNOW ABOUT WOMEN: Whether or not they have a clean credit record, a complete understanding of the infield fly rule, and a need to spend money to be "pampered."

ON MY NIGHTSTAND: Lamp, clock radio.

TIME ON MY HAIR/MY LOOK: Five minutes/I'm trying to achieve the illusion of three dimensions.

COMFORTWEAR: Golf shoes.

BOYHOOD DREAM: I literally wanted to be a game-show host when I grew up. Preferably, Bob Goen.

FREE ADVICE: You can do anything you want in life. Just dream it, then go do it.

FAVORITES:

BOOK: *Death in Venice.*

MOVIE: *Cinderella Liberty.*

TV SHOW: *The Wonder Years.*

MAGAZINE: *The Sporting News.*

CEREAL: I don't eat breakfast.

CAR: Mercedes Benz 450 SL.

SONG: tie: "Radar Love"—Golden Earring; "Tenderly"—Nat King Cole.

AFTER-SHAVE: Royal Copenhagen.

SPORT: To participate—golf; to watch—baseball.

SANDWICH: Hero.

DRINK: Absolut Gibson on the rocks, dry (with as many of those little onions as will fit on the stick).

NEWS ANCHOR: Ted Koppel.

SMOKE: My occasional Macanudo cigar.

ROBERT "BOB" GOULET, entertainer, Las Vegas, Nevada

Robert "Bob" Goulet is a classic Robert "Bob." He has an extremely deep voice that would be missed if ever Bob should leave us.

WHY I'M BOB: I didn't say I was a Bob. When I lived in Canada, everybody called me Bob. Then, during and after *Camelot*, I was Bobby. My present wife likes neither; so guess what: I'm now called Robert.

WHAT BEING BOB MEANS: A helluva lot more than Bubba.

MY GREAT WEEKEND: To be somewhere on a cliff, overlooking the sea with a bottle of good wine, some excellent food, my loved one by my side, and plenty of *Gomer Pyle* tapes.

BAD BOBS I'VE KNOWN: None yet!

I'M HANDY AT...: Opening the refrigerator door.

BEHAVIOR I DISLIKE: Stuffy, or that of those who think too much of themselves.

MY HELL ON EARTH: A bad marriage.

WHO I TRUST AND DISTRUST: My wife. Oh Lord, I used to trust everyone, but after a few personal and monetary losses I'm much more wary.

MOST IMPORTANT THINGS TO KNOW ABOUT WOMEN: You never really know. But all you need to know is to love and respect them.
ON MY NIGHTSTAND: Magazines, books, a TV clicker, and a cup of coffee.
TIME ON MY HAIR/MY LOOK: Very little. I just try to keep it out of my eyes.
COMFORTWEAR: Blue jeans, cotton sweaters, running shoes.
BOYHOOD DREAM: To be a gynecologist.
FREE ADVICE: Do everything in moderation except when it comes to showing your love to your fellowman.
FAVORITES:
BOOK: Poems of T. S. Eliot.
MOVIE: *On the Waterfront.*
MAGAZINE: *World Press Review.*
CEREAL: All-Bran.
CAR: Testarossa.
SONG: "The Star-Spangled Banner."
AFTER-SHAVE: Sea Breeze.
SPORT: Golf.
SANDWICH: Tuna fish.
DRINK: Iced tea.
NEWS ANCHOR: All three.
SMOKE: A good cigar.

BOB GUCCIONE, JR., editor/publisher, *Spin* magazine, New York City

Bob Guccione, Jr., is the son of Bob Guccione, Sr., editor and publisher of *Penthouse* magazine. Of the two, Bob Jr. is more Bob-like. He takes no responsibility for his father.
WHY I'M BOB: Bob is cool. Robert is too stuffy. "Bobby" took years to get away from, except for people who knew me at least ten years ago, for whom it's like a secret-society password. Robby and Rob are obviously for social misfits and this was obviously a trick question.
WHAT BEING BOB MEANS: Absolutely nothing at all.
MY GREAT WEEKEND: Saturday and Sunday. Okay—Thursday to Monday afternoon in Paris.
I'M HANDY AT...: Filling out questionnaires. Sometimes I make doctor's appointments just to fill out the questionnaires—and then leave before the doctor can call me.
BEHAVIOR I DISLIKE: Blatant flatulence, murder, bigotry—not necessarily in that order.
MY HELL ON EARTH: Getting stuck in an elevator with a homicidal bigot who has just eaten Mexican food.
WHO I TRUST AND DISTRUST: Trust: God. Don't: People who say they are sent by God to ask for money and to stamp out pornography and rock and roll.
MOST IMPORTANT THINGS TO KNOW ABOUT WOMEN: Men must be prepared to deliver all the same honesties that we demand from them.
ON MY NIGHTSTAND: Last night's half-drunk glass of water.
TIME ON MY HAIR/MY LOOK: About four or five hopeless minutes toweling it dry/awake.
COMFORTWEAR: Nothing.
BOYHOOD DREAM: To be a soccer player. This failure drove me to want to be one of the most important editors and publishers of my time. Seriously (though inexplicably).
FREE ADVICE: That life is too vast a mystery for any parent to pretend to have conquered, but, nonetheless, it doesn't hurt to ask for advice.
FAVORITES:
BOOK: *Peter Pan.*
MOVIE: *Lawrence of Arabia* and *Apocalypse Now.*
TV SHOW: *Monty Python.*
MAGAZINE: *Spin.*

CEREAL: Porridge.
CAR: Aston Martin Lagonda.
SONG: "Bridge over Troubled Water."
AFTER-SHAVE: None.
SPORT: Soccer.
SANDWICH: Grilled cheese and bacon.
DRINK: Wine.
NEWS ANCHOR: Dan Rather.

BOB HOPE, entertainer, Toluca Lake, California

Bob Hope was born Leslie Townes Hope, in Eltham, England. After coming to America (Cleveland), he changed his name for professional reasons and, in time, became King of the Bobs, the Biggest Bob of All, Bob "Hey, You'd Change Your Name Too If It Was Leslie" Hope. Besides being peerlessly famous among Bobs, Bob Hope is the most dependable entertainer we have. He works tirelessly. He isn't flashy. He golfs decently. He looks good in hats. He ages gracefully. He knows presidents. He owns Chryslers. He is The Bob, even if he was a Leslie.

WHY I'M BOB: When I started in vaudeville, I found myself starving in Chicago. In those days, I was Leslie Townes Hope. I couldn't get a date. Nobody would see my act. I had started in Cleveland, my hometown, where I was getting $10 a show. Then I played Detroit, for $10 a show. In Chicago, though, I couldn't get a date. I was just about ready to go back to Cleveland to get my laundry done and a full meal, when I decided to change my name. I thought, "Hey, Leslie's a girl's name! I think what I'll do is change it to Bob. It's more chummy; Bob Hope is more chummy than Leslie Hope. There's a little more warmth to it." Leslie had a little question mark behind it, you know? The next booking agent I went to see looked at me and said, "Would $25 a show be all right?" And I gulped. I said, "Yeah, that'll be fine." I mean, I'd been so hungry, I had just eaten my Adam's apple the night before. So I played three shows as Bob Hope and got hired down the street for $200 a week, then $250 a week! Big money, you know?

I was Bob. Never stopped after that.

WHAT BEING BOB MEANS: I can tell you a funny story about being Bob. Not long after this, I was going into Evanston, Illinois, to play a show. After rehearsal with the band, I went into the restaurant and had a little bite, and I checked the newspapers to see how they billed me. They had me as "Ben Hope." I took the paper to the manager of the theater and said, "What's the idea of putting 'Ben Hope' in this thing?"

He said, "Well, what's your name?"

I said, "My name is BOB Hope."

He said, "Who knows?"

I didn't have an answer for that. He was right. So I was Ben Hope for three days. Isn't that beautiful?

MY GREAT WEEKEND: I just had one: Friday night I went down to Palm Springs, stayed there, played golf, had dinner with a few friends, and watched a little television, which I don't get a chance to do much. Last night, I watched the Perry Mason thing. And yesterday afternoon, I watched golf. And I relaxed, you know?.

BAD BOBS I'VE KNOWN: No no no. I know a lot of Bobs. Bob Dole, the senator. I admire him. He's a war hero, you know. I like him.

I'M HANDY AT...: Shooting a par.

BEHAVIOR I DISLIKE: It all depends. Somebody being a little loud and abusive to a waitress or something. I drove up to Palm Springs one day and a guy cut me off—I wasn't driving; my man was driving, but he cut right in front of us, missing us just by inches. And I haven't liked him since. I don't know who he was, but I haven't liked him since.

MY HELL ON EARTH: When you're playing an exhibition golf course, which I did with Bing a lot of times, and you hit a great golf iron to the hole. And then you miss the three-foot putt. And the whole audience goes, "Ohhhhhh." You feel like crawling in the hole. That's hell on earth, I wanna tell ya.

WHO I TRUST AND DISTRUST: I trust a lot of people. I trust my cook. Both of my cooks.

MOST IMPORTANT THINGS TO KNOW ABOUT WOMEN: Oh, I don't know. Just their personality, I think. A study of their character. And maybe how well they sing. Dolores is still singing today as well as she did when I met her.

I'm never on guard with women, though. I've been associated with them so long that you know when to get away from somebody who's a little strange or something.

ON MY NIGHTSTAND: I have a bottle of Evian. Nothing important. I have my glasses, because when the paper comes up in the morning, the first thing I do is look at the headlines and see if there are any subjects I want to talk about in the monologue. In the drawer, under my phone, there are some sleeping pills, if I need them. I don't need them very often.

TIME ON MY HAIR/MY LOOK: That's funny. I just check to see if there's any there. I'm very careful with my hair. I brush it a lot. Isn't that funny you would ask that? It's a very important thing to me: I brush my hair to keep it in order.

COMFORTWEAR: I have a pair of corduroy jeans on now, a golf shirt, and white socks. I can slip right into my golf shoes very quickly.

BOYHOOD DREAM: I don't remember wanting to be anybody.

FREE ADVICE: Oh, I don't know. My wife did more good for my kids than I ever did. I was on the road. For instance, I was leaving again on a road trip one time, and I yelled over to Tony—he was eight years old—I said, "Goodbye, Tony." And he said, "Goodbye, Bob Hope." That made me do a take. I said, Wait a minute. But then later I started taking them with me.

FAVORITES:

BOOK: I tell ya, everybody sends me books. I have Nixon's book here. Eisenhower's book. What's his name on CNN—Larry King's too.

MOVIE: [OF HIS OWN] I liked *The Facts of Life,* which I did with Lucy. *Seven Little Foys,* too. And *Paleface.* I was sleeping with Trigger in that one, you know.

TV SHOW: I wouldn't miss *The Golden Girls*; I love them.

MAGAZINE: I have my own plane and my pilot puts *all* of them on the plane for me. Every magazine you can think of, and I read them.

CEREAL: Batman. Have you seen it? My cook bought a box for me. I keep it up in my office and I just nibble on it. It's good, isn't it? I don't think you can go too bad with that.
CAR: Chrysler, what else? I won a BMW worth $50,000 last week. I gave it back because, I said, "Lee Iacocca wouldn't like me in that."
SANDWICH: She makes bacon and cheese on toast, with a little tomatoes and stuff, on the grill, and I'm in heaven. I'd kill for that.
DRINK: I have one wine that I picked up in Michigan. Ford served it at the White House. It's a Michigan wine. Can you imagine that? I don't like a real dry wine; it doesn't mean anything to me. This is sort of a neutral wine.
AFTER-SHAVE: Water. Hot water. Then cold water.
SONG: "Thanks for the Memories."
NEWS ANCHOR: Walter Cronkite still. I trust him like my agent.

BOB KANE, creator of Batman, Los Angeles, California

In 1939 Bob Kane created Batman in his own image. Bob Kane rhymes with Bruce Wayne. Bob Kane owns a cape. Bob Kane is still a Bob.

WHY I'M BOB: Robert is too formal to sign on my comic strip. My Bronx cronies called me Robby, until I dropped it at age 18 when I created Batman. Bob sounded just right.
WHAT BEING BOB MEANS: That I was given the right name.
MY GREAT WEEKEND: Escaping to a secluded cottage at the beach with my beautiful wife, Elizabeth. Swimming, reading (not a comic book!), a candlelight supper, champagne. And no telephone calls, please!
I'M HANDY AT...: Obviously, my dear Watson, drawing pictures.
BEHAVIOR I DISLIKE: Dominating and exploitative, for material gain. Also I abhor liars, cheats, con artists, blowhards, and boorish people whom I avoid like the plague.
WHO I TRUST AND DISTRUST: I trust people who have proven their integrity and friendship when they come to your aid in time of crisis. I do not trust fair-weather friends who only show up at party time.
MOST IMPORTANT THINGS TO KNOW ABOUT WOMEN: They need compassion and understanding whenever they are at a crossroad. Women have a real need for communication.
ON MY NIGHTSTAND: Obviously a lamp and a pencil and pad—in case I get a creative idea in the middle of the night.
COMFORTWEAR: Old clothing: sweaters, jeans, sneakers.
BOYHOOD DREAM: I wanted to be a famous cartoonist and did not disappoint myself. For more on this subject, I suggest you read my autobiography, *Batman and Me*.
FREE ADVICE: Be forthright and honest.
FAVORITES:
BOOK: *Batman and Me* and *Les Misérables*.
MOVIE: *It's a Wonderful Life*.
TV SHOW: *Batman* (Am I being prejudiced? It was a most unique and original series.)
CEREAL: Oatbran Flakes (Frankly, I find them all boring and tasteless—ugh!).
CAR: Excaliber Convertible.
SONG: "The Song Is You" by Sinatra.
AFTER-SHAVE: Pierre Cardin.
SPORT: Stock-car racing, boxing.
SANDWICH: Hot dog with mustard and hot sauerkraut (to me, it's more delicious on first bite than caviar).
NEWS ANCHOR: Ted Koppel.
SMOKE: Occasionally a pipe.

BOB KEESHAN, Captain Kangaroo/child advocate, New York City

Bob Keeshan has been Captain Kangaroo since October 3, 1955. It is uncertain in what division of the military he serves.

WHY I'M BOB: It seems okay. There didn't seem any reason to change it. I honestly can't say I'm particularly enamored of it. Not that I dislike it—it's just what they gave me. It's worked well, so why change it? Ultimately, it's something to answer to when it's dinnertime. I don't think I'd be very different if I wasn't named Bob. Although if my mother called me Mortimer, I might be a very different person, having had to fight my way out of elementary school or something. Bobs don't have that problem.

WAS CAPTAIN KANGAROO'S FIRST NAME BOB: No, Captain was his first name. There was no need to go any further than that. It certainly wasn't going to be Captain Bob. There were 17,000 local personalities named Captain Bob or Jack or Mortimer—no, probably not a Mortimer.

MY GREAT WEEKEND: One where the telephone doesn't ring too much. A quiet weekend, where I can get away and do stuff. It could be catching up on reading, or taking the camera in the car for a little trip, or playing with my grandchildren.

BAD BOBS I'VE KNOWN: I haven't met a guy I didn't like, really. I don't waste my time not liking people. Maybe it's part of being an easygoing Bob. Maybe I've met a Bob I didn't approve of, but disliking takes too much effort. I'm not dubious; I'm Bob, actually.

I'M HANDY AT...: I think I can do things I know I can't do, and I keep repeating that mistake. "Oh, I can take care of that. No need to call the carpenter! No need to call the plumber!" Then I find out for the 7,000th time that life would have been a lot easier if I had called a plumber named Bill or Jack or Harry.

I guess it comes from an independence. We Bobs hate to be overly dependent on others. We like to manage our own fate. But it's important for us to recognize our limitations.

BEHAVIOR I DISLIKE: Absolute effusiveness and outgoingness. I don't mean occasionally; I mean all the time. I don't know how anybody keeps that up or what generates that kind of behavior.

MY HELL ON EARTH: In this business, you sometimes get involved in situations where you're with a lot of people that you wouldn't choose to be with. I might be out doing a lecture or a show and have to be involved with effusive people, for instance. They just drive you bananas. But there's nothing you can do about that. You've got to grow up and learn how to handle that.

WHO I TRUST AND DISTRUST: I trust just about anybody until proven otherwise—and that's probably dumb. I'm sure I've been taken advantage of many, many times.

MOST IMPORTANT THINGS TO KNOW ABOUT WOMEN: You've got to recognize they're different from men. And you've got to be considerate. A lot of guys in today's society are not particularly considerate of women.

ON MY NIGHTSTAND: An alarm clock, eyedrops for my contacts when I wake up in the morning, and not much else. Reading glasses, because I usually read in bed before I go to sleep. The book, however, doesn't go on the nightstand, which isn't big enough. The book goes on the floor. And that's there purposely so I can trip over it when getting up in the morning.

TIME ON MY HAIR/MY LOOK: I don't really care that much, except that I do spend a lot of time on it. I'm in a business where looks count, so it would be silly if I parted my hair on the right for one show and on the left for the next. I don't know if it's a look or not. Thank God I've got enough left to comb.

COMFORTWEAR: Chinos and a good-looking sports shirt. And sneakers. I live in walking shoes. I've got terrible feet. God, my feet hurt all the time.

BOYHOOD DREAM: To be a lawyer, but had to work at NBC to support myself. I became involved in television before there was a television, so by the time television grew up under me, the law plans were gone. For that, the American Bar Association can thank God.

FREE ADVICE: Be a nice person first and worry about being successful second. That will just come on its own. I've always espoused with my kids that personal happiness was far more important. They're good people, also successful; but good people.

FAVORITES:

MOVIE: *Treasure of the Sierra Madre*.

TV SHOW: *Andy Griffith*; I think he's a terrific guy; I always relax watching him.

MAGAZINE: I really don't read too many of them. I skim them in the dentist's office, but if I'm lucky I don't have to go to the dentist's office.

CEREAL: Some sort of flakes—I don't really care what kind, as long as there are bananas on top. I ignore the flakes and eat the banana.

CAR: I'm very fickle about cars.

AFTER-SHAVE: Nah, not really.

SPORT: If I were really forced to choose: baseball.

SANDWICH: Tuna fish.

DRINK: Is there anything better than water?

NEWS ANCHOR: You want me to commit suicide? I know most of them fairly well.

BOB MACKIE, designer, Los Angeles, California

Bob Mackie is the longtime master of TV fashion and Oscarwear. He dressed Diana Ross. He dressed Carol Burnett. He dresses Cher—when she wears clothes.

WHY I'M BOB: Because of an older "Cousin Robert," I became "little Bobby." When I was about 13, a more sophisticated "Bob" seemed more appropriate. Later on, after seeing my first screen credit as Robert Mackie, I quickly decided that Bob was less pretentious.

WHAT BEING BOB MEANS: Bob is a funny word or name and hopefully it conveys that I don't take myself all that seriously.

MY GREAT WEEKEND: Hanging out with my dogs, good friends, and plenty of good food.

I'M HANDY AT...: What?

BEHAVIOR I DISLIKE: Brown-nosing.

MY HELL ON EARTH: New York City in August.

WHO I TRUST AND DISTRUST: Trust: old best friends. Don't trust: new people who insist they're my best friends.

MOST IMPORTANT THING TO KNOW ABOUT WOMEN: Do they wear panty hose or a garter belt?

ON MY NIGHTSTAND: Clock, lamp, cookies, milk.

TIME ON MY HAIR/MY LOOK: Two minutes/youthful indifference.

COMFORTWEAR: Sweatshirt, khakis, Bass Weejun, with white socks.

BOYHOOD DREAM: I wanted to be Gene Kelly—I readjusted!

FREE ADVICE: Don't bullshit!
FAVORITES:
BOOK: *Gone With the Wind*, read at age 15.
MOVIE: *Singing in the Rain*, seen at age 12.
TV SHOW: *Masterpiece Theater*.
MAGAZINE: *Life* magazine in the 1940s and fifties.
CEREAL: None.
CAR: Mercedes.
AFTER-SHAVE: Never use it.
SPORT: Sleeping.
SANDWICH: Hot dog with mustard and relish.
DRINK: Vodka martini.
NEWS ANCHOR: Tom Brokaw.
SMOKE: No.

 BOB MARTWICK, animal handler (Morris the Cat), Lombard, Illinois

Bob Martwick lives with Morris the Cat. If Morris, the most finicky creature alive, can happily coexist with a Bob, anyone can.

WHY I'M BOB: My family and friends dictated it.
WHAT BEING BOB MEANS: Being satisfied at having had a meaningful and productive life.
MY GREAT WEEKEND: Relaxing with friends. Golf, boating—but not necessary.
BAD BOBS I'VE KNOWN: He was egotistical and self-centered.
I'M HANDY AT...: Training dogs, working with cats. Also handy with tools of various trades: carpentry, plumbing.
BEHAVIOR I DISLIKE: Aggressiveness, loudness, ill-mannered people.
MY HELL ON EARTH: Illness.
WHO I TRUST AND DISTRUST: I trust most people. I don't trust braggarts.
MOST IMPORTANT THING TO KNOW ABOUT WOMEN: How sincere are they?
ON MY NIGHTSTAND: Lamp, alarm clock, and early in the evening, maybe a beer.
TIME ON MY HAIR/MY LOOK: One minute. I have maintained a service "flattop" since World War II.
COMFORTWEAR: Pants, sports shirt, sweater.
BOYHOOD DREAM: To be a pilot in the naval air corps.
FREE ADVICE: Be honest, fair, and love your family.
FAVORITES:
BOOK: *Lawrence of Arabia*.
MOVIE: *Lawrence of Arabia*.
TV SHOW: None.
MAGAZINE: *National Geographic*.
CEREAL: Shredded Wheat.
CAR: One that's running.
SONG: "Ragtime Cowboy Joe."
AFTER-SHAVE: Old Spice.
SPORT: Football.
SANDWICH: Sardine.
DRINK: Whatever.
NEWS ANCHOR: Lowell Thomas.
SMOKE: Never.

BOB McGRATH, *Sesame Street* regular, New York City

On *Sesame Street*, Bob McGrath is known only as Bob. To children around the world, he needs no last name.

WHY I'M BOB: I gave up Bobby when I reached puberty. Sometimes I use my first and second name together, Robert Emmet, because he was a famous Irish patriot.

WHAT BEING BOB MEANS: It's very meaningful to me to be Bob, because that's my name on *Sesame Street*. No one knows my last name. To the kids and their parents who watch the show, I'm just plain Bob, except for a number of two-year-olds who call me Bop.

MY GREAT WEEKEND: Since I often end up performing my live concerts on the weekends, my idea of a great weekend is a full house and a great show.

BAD BOBS I'VE KNOWN: None, but I'd be happy to meet one.

I'M HANDY AT...I'm a full-time household handyman. I do pretty much everything from cleaning gutters to growing roses to making furniture to photographing my new grandchild. I also make fantastic *"sesame seed"* pancakes.

BEHAVIOR I DISLIKE: It takes a lot to make me uncomfortable. Let's face it, I spend my days with a six-foot yellow bird and a grouch in a trash can.

MY HELL ON EARTH: Walking out onstage in front of a full house and realizing I don't have a clue what music is being played.

WHO I TRUST AND DISTRUST: I'm a trusting person.

MOST IMPORTANT THINGS TO KNOW ABOUT WOMEN: In my house, the most important thing to know about women, especially my daughters, is keeping their names straight.

ON MY NIGHTSTAND: I'm probably the only Bob in the whole world that does not have a nightstand.

TIME ON MY HAIR/MY LOOK: I spend just the right amount of time on my hair. I'm trying to achieve something between Pee Wee Herman and Mel Gibson.

COMFORTWEAR: Work clothes and my wedding ring.

BOYHOOD DREAM: I thought I was going to be a mechanical engineer.

FREE ADVICE: I have five children. I tell them be as well-prepared as you can possibly be for everything.

BOOK: *Love in the Time of Cholera*.

TV SHOW: *The Wonder Years*.

CEREAL: Irish oatmeal.

CAR: Any German car.

AFTER-SHAVE: None.

SPORT: Football.

SANDWICH: Pastrami.

DRINK: Dr. Brown's Cream Soda.

NEWS ANCHOR: Bill Moyers.

THE HONORABLE BOB MILLER,
Governor of Nevada, Carson City, Nevada

Bob Miller is, for the moment, the only governor named Bob.

WHY I'M BOB: In 1975, I was appointed justice of the peace. The following year I had to seek election to retain my position. That required me to decide how my name would appear on the ballot. I thought Robert sounded the most judicial, and so it remained until one hour before the close of filing when I was informed of the candidacy of another Robert Miller. I hastily became Bob, and he left on vacation for Bermuda. I've been Bob ever since.

WHAT BEING BOB MEANS: It means you're approachable and down-to-earth, and when you show up backward no one knows.

MY GREAT WEEKEND: Playing basketball with my son and daughter.

I'M HANDY AT...: Getting up in the morning and being Bob.

MY HELL ON EARTH: Being locked in a room with people who are stuffy and aloof.

WHO I TRUST AND DISTRUST: I trust the wife and kids and anyone named Bob. I don't trust everyone else, but especially those who go by the name Robert.

MOST IMPORTANT THING TO KNOW ABOUT WOMEN: That you really don't know anything.

ON MY NIGHTSTAND: Book, clock radio, TV remote, and various thingamabobs.

TIME ON MY HAIR/MY LOOK. Fifteen minutes/Wavy, Somewhat Discombobulated look.

COMFORTWEAR: Levi's or shorts, golf shirts, tennis shoes.

BOYHOOD DREAM: To be the star of any pro team. Kareem Abdul Jabar.

FREE ADVICE: Be organized, trustworthy, and honest.

FAVORITES:

BOOK: *True Story of the Three Little Pigs* by A. Wolf.

MOVIE: *The Great Race.*

TV SHOW: *Maverick.*

MAGAZINE: *Sports Illustrated.*

CEREAL: Raisin Squares.

CAR: Lincoln Town Car.

SONG: "Venus" by Frankie Avalon.

AFTER-SHAVE: Brut.

SPORT: Basketball.

SANDWICH: Cold turkey with horsey sauce and sweet pickles.

DRINK: Diet Coke.

NEWS ANCHOR: Bob Schieffer.

BOB NEWHART, comedian, Los Angeles, California

When former accountant Bob Newhart is greeted, he is usually greeted, "Hi, Bob." On his first sitcom, *The Bob Newhart Show* (1972–78), he played Dr. Bob Hartley, a Chicago psychologist whose friends greeted him constantly. Later, Newhart starred in his second sitcom, *Newhart* (1982–90), on which he portrayed an innkeeper named Dick, who looked very much like a Bob. Bob claims to have a name in mind for his next series. "This one's gotta be *Bob*," predicts Bob. "It's the only thing we have left."

WHY I'M BOB: I was born George Robert. Which means I'm George to people I was in the service with. And I'm legally still George, but I've been called Bob since high school. My friends call me Bob. There was a saying, "Let George do it." I figured I was going to be asked to do a lot of things I wouldn't want to do, so I thought, "Maybe I'll be a Bob."

WHAT BEING BOB MEANS: I never made the connection that Bobs tend to be an island of calmness in a sea of discord. I always say, however, of the characters I play, "He's convinced he's the last sane man on the earth." Maybe being a Bob has something to do with this. When people see me on the street, all guys think I look like somebody who was in the service with them and all the women think I look like their first husband. They come up to me with, "Where the hell's the check?" Then they realize they've made a mistake, and they back off. There was a *GE Theater* movie years ago with Jack Benny, playing a man with a face nobody could remember. A crime was committed and none of the witnesses could identify him because he has that kind of nondescript face. He never stood out in a crowd. And that always stuck with me.

MY GREAT WEEKEND: During the week I get out to play golf, but we have an unspoken rule that the weekends be put aside to spend with the family.

BAD BOBS I'VE KNOWN: Hmm, there was a Bob the Terrible, a Russian Czar, a little-known figure in history. Aside from him, I don't think so.

I'M HANDY AT...: I'm good with electronic equipment. With VCRs and computers. I know how they work.

BEHAVIOR I DISLIKE: People's indifference to other people. That upsets me. People who go through red lights. I have imaginary conversations with those people. We all have to play by the same rules, otherwise it's a jungle out there.

MY HELL ON EARTH: Filling out a questionnaire like this one.

WHO I TRUST AND DISTRUST: I trust my friends, certainly. I distrust people whose word wasn't good.

MOST IMPORTANT THINGS TO KNOW ABOUT WOMEN: The difference. You can't equate them to men. We're logical and they're emotional, and we tend to deal with them logically while they tend to deal with us emotionally.

ON MY NIGHTSTAND: An alarm clock set for 7:30 when my daughter Courtney goes to school.

TIME ON MY HAIR/MY LOOK: Probably thirty seconds. The look I'm trying to achieve is full. And I'm not successful. So far I'm not losing ground. It's in a holding pattern.

COMFORTWEAR: Probably cords. I guess I wear them 90 percent of the time. A golf shirt.

BOYHOOD DREAM: Certainly not what I'm doing today. Probably to be in some peripheral form of show business, like advertising. Something very pragmatic, with a weekly check.

FREE ADVICE: It's all right to make mistakes. The whole world isn't riding on you. We all make mistakes.

FAVORITES:
BOOK: Sherlock Holmes; anything by Robert Benchley.
MOVIE: *Dr. Strangelove.*
TV SHOW: *Buffalo Bill.*
MAGAZINE: *The Atlantic.*
CEREAL: None—toast and jam.
CAR: My Dodge van.
SONG: "Little Darling" by Count Basie.
AFTER-SHAVE: None.
SPORT: Boxing, golf.
SANDWICH: French dip, but only on my birthday.
DRINK: Pepsi.

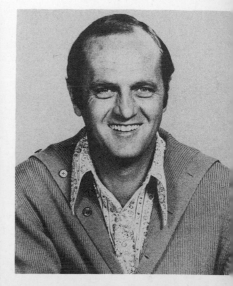

BOB RICHARDS, Olympic champion/public speaker, Minneapolis, Minnesota

Bob Richards is Mr. Wheaties. He has been Mr. Wheaties since he won Olympic gold medals for pole vaulting in 1952 and 1956.

WHY I'M BOB: Bob was a better name for recognition. During my Olympic and other track-and-field competition, I was always called Bob. When I became spokesperson for Wheaties, they used the Bob Richards signature. For all my speaking engagements and personal appearances, I am known as Bob. Internationally I am known as Bob Richards.

WHAT BEING BOB MEANS: It's just a good common name.

MY GREAT WEEKEND: Time spent with my family, watching my kids compete in track and field or competing in sports myself. I'd have to include singing—I love to sing.

BAD BOBS I'VE KNOWN: I've known lots of 'em! But I don't want to name them.

I'M HANDY AT...: Just about everything. I guess they call that a jack of all trades and master of none!

BEHAVIOR I DISLIKE: Any real intense selfishness or dictatorial behavior. Any total lack of concern for others—totally self-centered people. Traits of megalomania.

MY HELL ON EARTH: Being locked in a truck or airplane or car and driving forever.

WHO I TRUST AND DISTRUST: I trust in God, ultimately—and some close personal friends. I don't trust power-mad capitalists, monopolists, or politicians.

MOST IMPORTANT THING TO KNOW ABOUT WOMEN: Mainly, treat them as equals—but thank God for the difference!.

ON MY NIGHTSTAND: A clock. My pajamas during the day, my work clothes during the night.

TIME ON MY HAIR/MY LOOK: Practically nothing—the less the better. I prefer a short cut and might add a little dye, especially for pictures.

COMFORTWEAR: T-shirts, Levi's.

BOYHOOD DREAM: I wanted to be Albert Schweitzer. He is the greatest man that ever lived. I can add Jesse Owens and Dutch Warmerdam as people I wanted to be like. I wanted to be a motivator of people and to do something for humanity.

FREE ADVICE: I have six children. All you really have to pass on to the next generation is your kids, and we should all spend a lot more time with our kids. My philosophy is work hard and go to school, and then go for your dreams. Be normal, live a clean and healthy life without drugs or alcohol, and treat other people fairly.

FAVORITES:

BOOKS: *Living Philosophers* by Will Durant; *Critique of Pure Reason* by I. Kant; Dialogues of Plato; Spinoza's books; *Out of My Life and Thoughts* by Schweitzer; Emerson's *Essays*.

MOVIE: None.

TV SHOW: PBS educational and comedy shows.

MAGAZINE: *Time*.

CEREAL: Wheaties and Cheerios.

CAR: 1980 Cadillac and Mercedes.

SONGS: "Riding Down the Canyon to See the Sun Go Down"; "In the Evening by the Moonlight"; "With Someone Like You"; "Home on the Range"; "Lyda Rose"; *The Music Man*—all the music.

AFTER-SHAVE: None.

SPORT: Track and field.

SANDWICH: Club or hamburger.

DRINK: Milk.

NEWS ANCHOR: I watch all three.

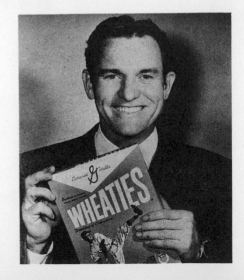

BOB SAGET, comedian/actor, Los Angeles, California

Bob Saget is a stand-up comedian who is a cast member of the ABC-TV sitcom *Full House*, and is the host of *America's Funniest Home Videos* on the same network.

WHY I'M BOB: Bob seemed okay. My last name was the hard one to grow up with.

WHAT BEING BOB MEANS: To see another Bob is very exciting. It's like driving down the street and seeing a car that's the same make and color as yours. You just want to honk and yell, "Yeah!"

MY GREAT WEEKEND: Lying around and playing with my wife and kids. Actually, I play with my kids, and when my kids are too tired to play, I play with my wife. I'm talking adultlike tactile friction.

BAD BOBS I'VE KNOWN: One doesn't come to mind.

I'M HANDY AT...: Installing phone lines in the house (whoa!) and programming most electronic equipment (hold me back!). I also know who to call when I've screwed up the phone lines and electronic equipment.

BEHAVIOR I DISLIKE: Aloofness. Jealousy. Insecurity, Bitterness. And other qualities I occasionally possess.

MY HELL ON EARTH: When people you love are suffering or in pain. When total morons are in powerful positions. Playing the Catskills right after dinner.

WHO I TRUST AND DISTRUST: I trust my wife, friends, and family. I don't trust my wife, friends, and family when they're conspiring against me.

MOST IMPORTANT THINGS TO KNOW ABOUT WOMEN: That they're the most wonderful, beautiful things put on this earth and I'm not just saying that because they can completely control and dominate my every breath.

ON MY NIGHTSTAND: Magazines I haven't had time to read, phone, clock radio, lamp, Kleenex, stun gun, hatchet, and handcuffs... sorry, just kidding, no Kleenex.

TIME ON MY HAIR/MY LOOK: A few minutes to dry it/Trying to achieve dry hair.

COMFORTWEAR: A nursing bra. Actually: sneakers, T-shirts, running pants, and a very high turban (that matches my nursing bra).

BOYHOOD DREAM: I wanted to grow up to be like my childhood doctor in Norfolk, Virginia, Jerry Perlman. He was my hero and came to check on me after I was almost hit by a car, as a kid. My mom was panicked but he and I both knew I was fine. He was hip.

FAVORITES: (this week)
BOOK: *The Grapes of Wrath.*
MOVIE: *It's a Wonderful Life.*
TV SHOW: *Wiseguy.*
MAGAZINE: *Newsweek.*
CEREAL: NutriGrain.
CAR: BMW 535 and 750.
SONG: "Marie" by Randy Newman.
AFTER-SHAVE: Sea Breeze.
SPORT: Weightlifting.
SANDWICH: Corned beef, once or twice a year.
DRINK: OJ and cranberry mixed.
NEWS ANCHOR: Tom Brokaw.
SMOKE: A good cigar—but not the same one—a few times a year.

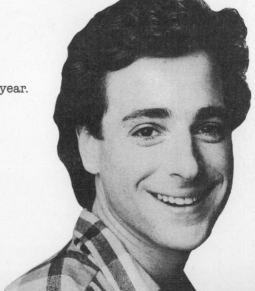

ROBERT "BOB" URICH, actor, Los Angeles, California

Robert "Bob" Urich was *Spenser for Hire*, as well as Dan Tana in *Vegas*. He was also Bob in the short-lived TV version of *Bob & Carol & Ted & Alice*.

WHY I'M BOB: It's not that I've abandoned Robert completely, but Bob is just a friendlier, more approachable guy than Robert! Besides, every Halloween when the kids get out the tub of water and those apples, my name comes up a lot!

WHAT BEING BOB MEANS: That I'm in great company!

MY GREAT WEEKEND: Being outside! Skiing, sailing, camping, fishing! And always with the people I care about!

BAD BOBS I'VE KNOWN: None.

I'M HANDY AT...: Making great pancakes on Sunday morning!

BEHAVIOR I DISLIKE: That of judgmental people who try to put you on the defensive.

MY HELL ON EARTH: A cocktail party: with people I know, it's merely uncomfortable; with people I don't know, it's sheer hell on earth.

WHO I TRUST AND DISTRUST: I trust a couple of close friends. I don't trust doctors, lawyers.

MOST IMPORTANT THING TO KNOW ABOUT WOMEN: They are different from men!

ON MY NIGHTSTAND: Don't have one! I use the floor! Lots of books, magazines, bottles of water.

TIME ON MY HAIR/MY LOOK: Thirty seconds to half a minute! No time at all!

COMFORTWEAR: Sweat clothes!

BOYHOOD DREAM: To be Hopalong Cassidy.

FREE ADVICE: Work up to your potential. Leave the trail cleaner than you found it! Love is the foundation for a successful life!

FAVORITES:

BOOK: *The Float Plane Notebook*.

MOVIE: *Midnight Cowboy*.

TV SHOW: *I Love Lucy*.

CEREAL: Cornflakes.

CAR: Ford Mustang.

SONG: "How High the Moon."

AFTER-SHAVE: Whatever I find in the medicine cabinet.

SPORT: Golf.

SANDWICH: Turkey on sourdough, with dijon and tomato.

DRINK: Water from a clean stream!

NEWS ANCHOR: Walter Cronkite.

BOB VILA, builder/TV host, Oyster Harbor, Massachusetts

Bob Vila is the former host of the PBS series *This Old House*. Currently he hosts the syndicated *Home Again, With Bob Vila*. He works with tools.

WHY I'M BOB: It was an effortless nondecision, typically Bob-like. It helps balance the Vila by its blandness.

WHAT BEING BOB MEANS: People do a quicker fix on Bobs than on Joes and Jacks.

MY GREAT WEEKEND: Just my wife and I. Sun, hot temps, water, sail, ski. Great cuisine. Someplace easy to get to.

BAD BOBS I'VE KNOWN: Some, but it had nothing to do with their Bobness.

I'M HANDY AT...: Loading and unloading the dishwasher.

BEHAVIOR I DISLIKE: Loud, pushy, disrespectful behavior.

MY HELL ON EARTH: Getting stuck on an ocean cruise with a thousand other people.

WHO I TRUST AND DISTRUST: I trust my friends and family. I don't trust my ex-employers.

MOST IMPORTANT THINGS TO KNOW ABOUT WOMEN: How to treat them respectfully and let them know how important a part of your life they are.
ON MY NIGHTSTAND: A lamp, a clock, and a phone.
TIME ON MY HAIR/MY LOOK: I wash it every day. Dry it in the winter and trim it every month. Lately, I watch it turn gray.
COMFORTWEAR: Khakis and a sweater.
BOYHOOD DREAM: To be an architect.
FREE ADVICE: Express your love, never hide it. Always be honest. Keep clean, wear a smile, and give others the respect you hope to get from them.
FAVORITES:
BOOK: *Bonfire of the Vanities.*
MOVIE: Anything with Michelle Pfeiffer in it.
TV SHOW: Mine.
MAGAZINE: *Rolling Stone.*
CEREAL: Mueslix.
CAR: 74 XKE V12.
SONG: "Let It Be."
AFTER-SHAVE: Guerlain Impérial.
SPORT: Cycling.
SANDWICH: Reuben, but I gave them up.
DRINK: La Mission Hautbrion '61.
NEWS ANCHOR: Walter Cronkite, Ralph Rennick.

BOB WEATHERWAX, Lassie's owner/trainer, Canyon Country, California

Bob Weatherwax's father, Rudd, was Lassie's original trainer. Bob inherited the leash and Lassie's progeny.

WHY I'M BOB: People are more comfortable with Bob.

WHAT BEING BOB MEANS: It means when you're in a crowd and someone yells "Bob," you can always count on one or several people looking up.

MY GREAT WEEKEND: Taking my sports cruiser boat out to Catalina for the weekend.

BAD BOBS I'VE KNOWN: None.

I'M HANDY AT...: Training dogs.

BEHAVIOR I DISLIKE: Dishonesty.

MY HELL ON EARTH: Seeing all the children in the street with nothing to eat.

WHO I TRUST AND DISTRUST: I trust my animals. I do not trust the government.

MOST IMPORTANT THING TO KNOW ABOUT WOMEN: You can't trust them either.

ON MY NIGHTSTAND: A lamp and my TV clicker.

TIME ON MY HAIR/MY LOOK: Ten minutes/Professionally respected without losing the common touch.

COMFORTWEAR: Levi's, T-shirts, and tennies.

BOYHOOD DREAM: To be a trainer, like my father.

FREE ADVICE: You will only get out of life what you put into it.

FAVORITES:

BOOK: *The Man Who Would Be King*, Rudyard Kipling.

MOVIE: *The African Queen.*

TV SHOW: *M*A*S*H.*

MAGAZINE: *New Yorker.*

CEREAL: Wheat Chex.

CAR: BMW.

SONG: "Your Song," Elton John.

AFTER-SHAVE: Poco.

SPORT: Boxing.

SANDWICH: Cheeseburger.

DRINK: Screwdriver.

NEWS ANCHOR: Read newspapers.

SMOKE: Marlboro (attempting to quit).

BOB WELCH, Oakland A's pitcher, Oakland, California

In 1990, Bob Welch was the first 20-game winner in the majors. He went on to a 27-6 record, the best in baseball that year, and earned the American League Cy Young Award.

WHAT BEING BOB MEANS: You're always second in line.

MY GREAT WEEKEND: Play golf at 6:55 A.M., Saturday. Come home to be with kids. Leave room for dinner at 6:00 P.M. A great walk down Main Street in Seal Beach with our family and Mary Ellen attacks me at 9:00 P.M., Saturday night. (We spend the next day recovering.)

BAD BOBS I'VE KNOWN: None.

I'M HANDY AT...: Changing shitty diapers.

BEHAVIOR I DISLIKE: Loud drunkenness.

MY HELL ON EARTH: No food or shelter for families who have lost family members in an earthquake.

WHO I TRUST AND DISTRUST: Trust: my wife, my family. Don't trust: endless.

MOST IMPORTANT THING TO KNOW ABOUT WOMEN: Pay special attention to the one you're sleeping with.

ON MY NIGHTSTAND: Dust.

TIME ON MY HAIR/MY LOOK: Ten minutes/a full head of hair.

COMFORTWEAR: Nothing or shorts.

BOYHOOD DREAM: I wanted to be an astronaut.

FREE ADVICE: Faith, hope, love, and time.

FAVORITES:

BOOK: *Big Book* by Bill W.

MOVIE: *The Wizard of Oz.*

TV SHOW: *Winnie the Pooh and Piglet Hour.*

MAGAZINE: *Penthouse.*

CEREAL: Froot Loops.

CAR: Large off-road Blazer.

SONG: "Wind Beneath My Wings."

AFTER-SHAVE: Old Spice.

SPORT: Basketball.

SANDWICH: Palao's special.

DRINK: Bottled water.

NEWS ANCHOR: Len Matuszek.

SMOKE: None.

20 NOTABLE BOBS TAKE THE BOB SURVEY

Bob Balaban, actor/film director, New York City
WHY I'M BOB: Bob went well with Balaban, all those "B's." When I was an apprentice in summer stock, Ann B. Davis said she thought Bob Balaban was a great stage name, so I left it.
WHAT BEING BOB MEANS: It means that in any gathering of more than six people, two are named Bob.
FREE ADVICE: Don't forget your childhood, but don't forget to grow up.
MOVIE: *La Ronde.*
TV SHOW: *Leave It To Beaver.*
CAR: '58 Olds station wagon.
SPORT: Rushing.

Bob Baldwin, Jazz keyboard artist,
New Rochelle, New York
WHY I'M BOB: Bob seems to merit more respect. Bobby is for those clean-shaven kind of guys. Bob's more straight to the point. My Dad's name is Bob.
WHAT BEING BOB MEANS: For my music, Bob is less stuffy than Robert.
I'M HANDY AT...: I've been playing piano since I was four.
MOST IMPORTANT THINGS TO KNOW ABOUT WOMEN: Their sensitivity, peaks and valleys in their personalities; their continual desire for attention and acknowledgment. Their ability to love is endless.
TIME ON MY HAIR/MY LOOK: A clean cut, artsy and professional look all rolled into one.
COMFORTWEAR: Pastel colors, silk shirts, soft shoes, small diamond earring, black Stetson hat.
BOYHOOD DREAM: To be an accountant.
FREE ADVICE: You should pass along traditions.
CEREAL: Kellogg's Apple Jacks.
SANDWICH: Peanut butter and jelly.

Bob Bell, retired TV clown (Bozo for 23 years on Chicago's WGN-TV), Lake San Maros, California

WHY I'M BOB: Primarily it's easier to spell, however, some people are inclined to add an extra "O" when addressing me.
BAD BOBS I'VE KNOWN: Only two, both with the same name as mine. They were the subjects of endless lawsuits mistakenly addressed to me.
I'M HANDY AT...: Avoiding unnecessary work and most of the necessary stuff.
BEHAVIOR I DISLIKE: The incessant rattling of paper sacks in an otherwise quiet environment.
MY HELL ON EARTH: St. Louis on a very hot summer day.
WHO I TRUST AND DISTRUST: I trust a debtor who repays in cash. I distrust a used-car salesman, dead or alive, even if his name is Bob.
ON MY NIGHTSTAND: A reminder to check the obituary columns before getting out of bed.
TIME ON MY HAIR/MY LOOK: I spend only as long as it takes to clean it off the shower floor.
COMFORTWEAR: Golf shoes.
BOYHOOD DREAM: To be a rich, retired, sex addict with a harem of beautiful girls. Well, one out of three ain't bad, as it turned out.
FREE ADVICE: Do the best you can with respect for others and express the love you feel to those you love.
CEREAL: Total with raisins.
SONG: Anything by Marilyn McCoo or Vic Damone.
AFTER-SHAVE: None.
SANDWICH: Homemade cheeseburger.
DRINK: Moderately on the rocks.
SMOKE: Ashamedly too much.

Bob Boden, director ABC-TV daytime development, Los Angeles, California
WHY I'M BOB: It fits really well on a license plate.
MY GREAT WEEKEND: Watching game shows on TV, snuggling with my honey, and shopping with coupons.
BEHAVIOR I DISLIKE: People who think they can take advantage of you because you're a nice Bob.
WHO I TRUST AND DISTRUST: I trust my car to the man who wears the star, the big bright Texaco star. I don't trust anyone who works in a gas station.
MOST IMPORTANT THING TO KNOW ABOUT WOMEN: How much of your Bobness they can put up with.
BOYHOOD DREAM: To be a game-show host.

Bob Bookman, Hollywood agent, Creative Artists Agency, Los Angeles, California
WHAT BEING BOB MEANS: It's the ultimate existential state of being.
BEHAVIOR I DISLIKE: Sycophantic, foolish, egotistic, predatory, and boorish people.
MY HELL ON EARTH: An eternity with people I can't stand.
MOST IMPORTANT THING TO KNOW ABOUT WOMEN: They can never be named Bob.
TIME ON MY HAIR/MY LOOK: The minimum. Never thought about it.
MOVIE: *La Grande Illusion*.
TV SERIES: *Police Squad*.
SMOKE: Monte Cristo #3.

Bob Brown, editor/publisher, *Soldier of Fortune* magazine, Boulder, Colorado
WHAT BEING BOB MEANS: Apathy and indifference.
MY GREAT WEEKEND: Work at SOF offices, jog, pump iron.
BAD BOBS I'VE KNOWN: None; but I haven't met any I particularly liked either.
I'M HANDY AT...: Vacillating.
MY HELL ON EARTH: Watching Roseanne Barr for more than 30 seconds.
MOST IMPORTANT THINGS TO KNOW ABOUT WOMEN: As Lord Chesterfield said,
"The pleasure is fleeting, the posture disgusting, and the price exorbitant."
ON MY NIGHTSTAND: Nothing.
TIME ON MY HAIR/MY LOOK: None to both questions.
BOYHOOD DREAM: To be General Patton.
FREE ADVICE: Get the brats to move out of the house and support themselves as soon
as possible. The military is also a wise alternative. Always suspect lawyers, politicians,
and stockbrokers.
BOOK: *1001 Sexual Positions*.
MOVIE: *The Wild Bunch*.
TV SHOW: *Miami Vice*.
MAGAZINE: *Soldier of Fortune*.
CEREAL: Granola.
CAR: 1963 Vega hatchback with a souped-up engine.
SONG: "Ballad of the Green Berets."
SANDWICH: Tuna fish.
DRINK: Alcohol.
SMOKE: Skoal.

Robert "Bob" Christgau, *Village Voice* rock critic, New York City
WHAT BEING BOB MEANS: It means being as common as dirt and one-dollar bills.
I'M HANDY AT...: I've gotten pretty good with stereos.
BEHAVIOR I DISLIKE: Idle conversation about stuff they think I'm interested in.
MY HELL ON EARTH: Fusion.
MOST IMPORTANT THING TO KNOW ABOUT WOMEN: Chances are a woman is
better at making you think you are interesting her than you are at interesting her.
FREE ADVICE: Don't be afraid to work, have fun, or fight.
DRINK: Beer. Brand varies with mood.

**Bob Colacello, contributing editor, *Vanity Fair*, author of *HOLY TERROR: Andy Warhol
Close Up*, New York City**
WHY I'M BOB: Because nobody would call me Robert except my mother and Sylvia
Miles.
WHAT BEING BOB MEANS: Common.
MY GREAT WEEKEND: Bobsledding in Bobolice, Poland.
BAD BOBS I'VE KNOWN: Bob Dylan. He seemed more like a Sigmund.
I'M HANDY AT...: Bob-bob-bobbing along.
BEHAVIOR I DISLIKE: Mixing me up with Bob Guccione.
MY HELL ON EARTH: Interviewing Bobby De Niro.
MOST IMPORTANT THING TO KNOW ABOUT WOMEN: Whether or not they bob their
hair.
ON MY NIGHTSTAND: A porcelain bobolink.
TIME ON MY HAIR/MY LOOK: A lot; the Rob Lowe look.
COMFORTWEAR: Bobby sox.
BOYHOOD DREAM: To be Bobby Darin.

BOOK: *The Bobsey Twins.*
MOVIE: *Bob & Carol & Ted & Alice.*
TV SHOW: *The Bob Newhart Show.*
MAGAZINE: *Bobtown Pennsylvania Gazette.*
CEREAL: Grilled bobwhite.
CAR: Mercury Bobcat.
AFTER-SHAVE: Bob, by Estée Lauder;
she makes it especially for me.
DRINK: Rob Roy.
NEWS ANCHOR: Larry King.

Bob Dove, consultant to Republican Senate leader, Washington, D.C.
I'M HANDY AT...: Wallpapering.
BEHAVIOR I DISLIKE: Deception.
MY HELL ON EARTH: The House of Representatives.
WHO I TRUST AND DISTRUST: Trust: God. Don't trust: anyone who hasn't proved otherwise.
MOST IMPORTANT THING TO KNOW ABOUT WOMEN: No way can any man know.
BOYHOOD DREAM: To be a truck driver.
TV SHOW: *Roseanne.*
DRINK: Bourbon.
SMOKE: Cigar.

Bob Ezrin, record producer (Kiss, Alice Cooper), Sherman Oaks, California
WHY I'M BOB: It is a strong name, simple to remember, and spacesaving on a message pad. It has a certain explosive quality lacking in the other forms of the name.
WHAT BEING BOB MEANS: It means that one is trusty, intrepid, earthy, kind, and strong. It means, above all else, to be right.
BEHAVIOR I DISLIKE: Mincing. Overly familiar behavior. Nervousness or obvious self-consciousness. Drunkenness. Proselytizing. Overly vulgar.
MY HELL ON EARTH: Being locked in a room full of violinists. Being locked in a room full of accordionists. Being locked in a room full of sibilant people, all whispering. Being locked in a room.
WHO I TRUST AND DISTRUST: I trust most Peters, some Walters, the occasional George, and absolutely no Dans. I trust many Bills, all Brians; I am wary of all Davids, although Daves can sometimes be counted on to take a proper lunch order.
MOST IMPORTANT THINGS TO KNOW ABOUT WOMEN: Forget it. You can't know them.
ON MY NIGHTSTAND: A full-band shortwave radio.
FREE ADVICE: A penny saved is still just a penny.

Bob Falls, artistic director of Chicago's Goodman Theater, Chicago, Illinois
WHAT BEING BOB MEANS: People understand a Bob. We're such good listeners. We hear everyone's problems and have trouble expressing ours. Life is supposed to be simple for a Bob; complexity isn't accepted. A Bob also isn't supposed to be unhappy; cranky perhaps, but a smile should always be very close to the surface.
MY GREAT WEEKEND: Afternoon movies.
I'M HANDY AT...: I am handy around the kitchen. I make oat-bran muffins.
MY HELL ON EARTH: Being seated between two other Bobs on an airplane. I don't want to be forced into this kind of Bob bonding.
TIME ON MY HAIR/MY LOOK: Thirty seconds to glare in the mirror and say, "Oh, forget it."
BOYHOOD DREAM: To be Abe Lincoln.
MOVIE: *McCabe and Mrs. Miller.*

MAGAZINE: *People.*
CEREAL: Rice Krispies.
SONG: "Guess I'll Hang My Tears Out to Dry," by Sinatra.

Bob Gale, screenwriter/producer (*Back to the Future*), Los Angeles, California
WHAT BEING BOB MEANS: Being Bob means that you're not one to take life too seriously. After all, if I wanted to be serious, I'd be Robert. Bob means you want to have some fun. No neckties, no suits, no wingtips. Hey, maybe the biggest problem with the world is that there's never been a good world leader named Bob. On the other hand, maybe somebody named Bob is incapable of being a world leader—it's way too serious an occupation.
MY GREAT WEEKEND: Any weekend that includes a nap.
I'M HANDY AT...: I'm one of those maddening individuals who actually knows how to program his VCR.
ON MY NIGHTSTAND: Pictures of my wife and daughter, a lamp, and whatever comic books I plan to read before I go to bed.
BOYHOOD DREAM: I never much really wanted to grow up, and I've been trying to avoid that possibility ever since.
FREE ADVICE: You have to take responsibility for your life, you have ultimate control of your destiny, and as Doc Emmett Brown (in *Back to the Future*) says, "Your future is what you make it, so make it a good one."
BOOK: *Adventures of Huckleberry Finn.*
MOVIE: *My Darling Clementine.*
TV SHOW: *The Honeymooners.*
MAGAZINE: Superman comics.
AFTER-SHAVE: Tap water.
SANDWICH: Barbecued cheeseburger, with raw onion, tomato and lettuce, smothered with D. L. Jardine's Texas barbecue sauce.
NEWS ANCHOR: Walter Cronkite (I watch him in VCR reruns instead of new news).

Bob Garfield, National Public Radio humorist, Burke, Virginia
WHY I'M BOB: Bob communicates approachability, self-possession, humility, and a better-than-average shot at the Publishers' Clearing House sweepstakes.
WHAT BEING BOB MEANS: It means never having to say you're Solly.

MY GREAT WEEKEND: Sitting in my underwear and eating hard pretzels while watching the ballgame. (No more than four beers for NFL game or three beers for major-league baseball. Moderation is an important part of being Bob.)

BAD BOBS I'VE KNOWN: Most of the people I don't like are named Nick.

I'M HANDY AT...: I can unscrew any jar with simple wrist action.

MY HELL ON EARTH: Rotary.

MOST IMPORTANT THINGS TO KNOW ABOUT WOMEN: If they read *Cosmopolitan*, watch *Oprah*, or bake for the church, they are normal and uninteresting and couldn't possibly be pretty enough to bother with. If they read newspapers, laugh at Woody Allen, and know how to swear, their looks are immaterial—even if they order whiskey sours in restaurants.

ON MY NIGHTSTAND: A 20-percent full bottle of Wart-X.

FREE ADVICE: For my daughters: Be nice, read. Do not have sex until I've been clinically dead for at least five years.

BOOK: *Miss Lonelyhearts* and *The Day of the Locust*.

MOVIE: *King Rat.*

TV SHOW: *Sesame Street.*

MAGAZINE: *New Yorker.*

NEWS ANCHOR: Charles Kuralt.

SMOKE: Most 70-cent cigars.

Bob Knoll, head of Auto Test Division of *Consumer Reports* magazine, Hadlyme, Connecticut

MY GREAT WEEKEND: Attending a sports-car race.

MY HELL ON EARTH: Being forced to drive a Chrysler K Car forever.

WHO I TRUST AND DISTRUST: I don't trust Lee Iacocca.

FREE ADVICE: No one gives you anything.

CAR: Mercedes 300/4Matic.

SPORT: Car racing.

AFTER-SHAVE: Old Spice.

Bob Kowalski, Author of *Eight-Week Cholesterol Cure* (says Bob, not sheepishly: "This book introduced oat bran to the American diet"), Venice, California

WHAT BEING BOB MEANS: A Bob is a friend for life. I've never known a Bob to beat his wife or torture his children.

BEHAVIOR I DISLIKE: I dislike both extremes of the human condition: the ultra-elitist intellectual snob who can't ever enjoy drinking a beer out of the can and the guy who, on the other hand, is closed to new ideas and who scoffs at those who savor a glass of fine wine.

MOST IMPORTANT THINGS TO KNOW ABOUT WOMEN: Whether they love children, flowers, food, and a sensuous life-style; and whether they can balance all those things along with a meaningful career and be able to enjoy the total package with a man.

BOYHOOD DREAM: Like most kids, I first wanted to be like my dad—a pharmacist in Chicago.

FREE ADVICE: Success is nothing if it doesn't include humanity.

CEREAL: Oat bran.

SANDWICH: Buffalo burgers.

DRINK: Beefeater martini.

Bob Mathias, Olympic decathlon gold medalist, Fresno, California

I'M HANDY AT...: All kinds of yardwork.

WHO I TRUST AND DISTRUST: Don't trust coach George Allen.

MOST IMPORTANT THING TO KNOW ABOUT WOMEN: Try to figure out what they are thinking.

TIME ON MY HAIR/MY LOOK: No look, just neat.
COMFORTWEAR: Work clothes.
FREE ADVICE: Do the best you can.
TV SHOW: *Mission Impossible*.
CAR: Ford pickup.
SONG: "Okie from Muskogee."
SPORT: Football.

Bob McAllister, former host of TV's *Wonderama*, New York City

WHY I'M BOB: As long as I can remember I've been called Bob. It fits me!
WHAT BEING BOB MEANS: It means everybody knows how to spell your name!
MY GREAT WEEKEND: Playing, good fun, good sex, good magic, family, roller skating around NYC!
I'M HANDY AT...: Entertaining kids!
ON MY NIGHTSTAND: Everything!
TIME ON HAIR/MY LOOK: Five minutes/a well-coiffed head!
BOYHOOD DREAM: To be me, Bob McAllister, only richer!
FREE ADVICE: Live by the Golden Rule!
MOVIE: *A Thousand Clowns*.
SONG: "Kids Are People Too."
SPORT: Sex.
DRINK: Milk.

Bob McAllister

Bob McGuire, host of *Bob McGuire's Outdoor Journal*, Johnson City, Tennessee

MY GREAT WEEKEND: Accomplishments and decisions without interruptions. Low stress (business is closed).
BAD BOBS I'VE KNOWN: I don't like Bobs when they become Roberts.
I'M HANDY AT...: From my wife's perspective, drying dishes. From my perspective, I can fix anything.
BEHAVIOR I DISLIKE: A soft smile with a hard lie.
MY HELL ON EARTH: The inability to achieve realistic objectives or being stuck in an elevator between floors for two hours with Oral Roberts. (Not a Bob!)
MOST IMPORTANT THING TO KNOW ABOUT WOMEN: The type of men they like.
BOOK: *National Geographic 100-Year Special*.
MOVIE: *Prancer*.
TV SHOW: *Nova*.
CEREAL: Cornflakes.
AFTER-SHAVE: Carrington.
SPORT: Wrestling—the real thing, no TV rasslin'.
DRINK: Wild Turkey and 7-Up.

Bob "Bob 1" Mothersbaugh, first of two Bobs in rock group Devo, Hollywood, California

WHY I'M BOB: Probably because it has less syllables.
WHAT BEING BOB MEANS: It means my Midwest roots are showing.
MY GREAT WEEKEND: Being somewhere besides L.A.
BAD BOBS I'VE KNOWN: In elementary school, Bob Oswald. We called each other BM and BO. Then we would fight.
WHO I TRUST AND DISTRUST: Me. Me.
ON MY NIGHTSTAND: Half a can of Bud.
COMFORTWEAR: Energy dome.
BOYHOOD DREAM: To be a veterinarian/cartoonist.
FREE ADVICE: Do as I say, not as I do.
BOOK: *Elvis Aaron Presley*.
MOVIE: *Jailhouse Rock* and *Freaks*.
AFTER-SHAVE: Tap water.

Bob Mould, musician, Burbank, California

WHY I'M BOB/WHAT BEING BOB MEANS: My grandmother called me Robby, my family called me Robert. With that in mind I guess it was an act of rebellion. I do not like being called Bub, however.

MY GREAT WEEKEND: Not answering the phone, not owing any money, not having anywhere definite to go.

I'M HANDY AT...: Working with my hands, trying to make them do the things I'm hearing in my head. I don't play sports anymore, afraid of breaking my hands, then everything would be stuck in my head.

MY HELL ON EARTH: I'm only part of a book, not a whole book, therefore I won't open up this rather large can of worms.

MOST IMPORTANT THINGS TO KNOW ABOUT WOMEN: They're different and they have feelings too. I guess they're different feelings than the ones I have.

TIME ON MY HAIR/MY LOOK: About 10 seconds a day. My hair is the least of my worries.

COMFORTWEAR: Nondescript clothing suits me best. I don't like standing out in a crowd. I don't need to look different, just see things differently.

BOYHOOD DREAM: I wanted to be a musician or a writer and now people tell me I am, so I'm lucky.

FREE ADVICE: Fathers should expect their children to be completely unlike them on the surface and exactly like them inside.

MOVIE: *Faster Pussycat, Kill Kill.*

TV SHOW: *The Simpsons.*

CEREAL: Granola with wheat germ and raisins.

CAR: Cars are functional.

SONG: The last one I'm working on; mine or someone's I'm working with.

DRINK: Water.

SANDWICH: Tuna with provolone on whole-wheat.

Bob Payton, Chicago-style restaurateur in Europe, Stapelford Park, Leicestershire, England

WHAT BEING BOB MEANS: Bob is okay. There are no hostile people named Bob. Bob is a happy name, a bouncy name, a name that is often confused with the great Do-Wop songs of the fifties like "B-Bob-Alula" or "Who Put the Bob in the Bob-shoo-Bob-shoo-Bob."

MY GREAT WEEKEND: My idea of a great weekend is to spend it with Bob and Wendy Payton at their Stapelford Park Country House Hotel in sunny Leicestershire. A brochure has been enclosed.

BAD BOBS I'VE KNOWN: I've never met a Bob I didn't like. Bobs that are Geminis I get on particularly well with. Bob Rabinowitz did break my nose playing basketball when I was in high school. However, I got over it and got a new nose at the same time.

I'M HANDY AT...: I'm handy at editing song-and-dance tapes to amuse myself.

BEHAVIOR I DISLIKE: I'm intolerant of incompetence and don't suffer fools gladly.

MY HELL ON EARTH: The thought of not being able to have a decent pizza or a good rare cheeseburger when I want it.

MOST IMPORTANT THINGS TO KNOW ABOUT WOMEN: They're not like men no matter how hard they try or no matter how much they think they are. They are more fun to be with than men are, even men named Bob.

ON MY NIGHTSTAND: Video player, *TV Guide*, empty glass of Diet Coke, Rolaids, glasses.
FREE ADVICE: Try and get out of this thing with your sanity intact.
MAGAZINE: *Country Life*.
CEREAL: Cheerios.
SPORT: Fox hunting.
SANDWICH: Rare cheeseburger.
DRINK: Diet Coke.

Tomato Bob Polenz, celebrated tomato farmer/actor, Stockton, New Jersey
WHY I'M BOB: I stuck with Bob because it goes best with Tomato. Tomato Robert doesn't do it.
WHAT BEING BOB MEANS: It means to be blond, fair with blue eyes, a belly that is a touch soft, and to have an open friendly attitude toward life and the living.
I'M HANDY AT...: Growing tomatoes, playing honky-tonk piano.
BEHAVIOR I DISLIKE: Clients not paying their bills.
MY HELL ON EARTH: A dry spring and wet summer, which ruins and rots tomato plants. Or, an audience holding those rotten tomatoes.
WHO I TRUST AND DISTRUST: I trust the spirit in us all. I don't trust a tomato, in any supermarket, that says "vine-ripened.'
COMFORTWEAR: A Tomato Bob T-shirt.
BOYHOOD DREAM: To be a famous singer. I am a singer, but I'm only famous for my tomatoes.
FREE ADVICE: There is more to life than hard work. Even with the most challenging weather, a tomato grows effortlessly. So shall we.
BOOK: *Burpee Seed Catalog*.
SONG: "I'll Never Leave You," by Harry Nilsson.
SANDWICH: Tomato and mayonnaise on fresh French bread with pepper.

Bob Schieffer, CBS News chief Washington correspondent, Washington, D.C.
WHY I'M BOB: My name *is* Bob, not Robert. My mom doesn't know why she chose Bob instead of Robert, she just did. She liked it fine, and so do I.
I'M HANDY AT...: Filling in for Dan Rather when he's in Berlin or Beijing or Moscow or wherever.
TIME ON MY HAIR/MY LOOK: Less and less.
SONG: "As Time Goes By."

Bob Shea, historical novelist, science fiction author, Glencoe, Illinois

WHY I'M BOB: I chose my own nickname as a preemptive measure after meeting a Robert known as Bobo. Yuck!

WHAT BEING BOB MEANS: I think of someone who is tall, slender, possessed of rugged good looks, active, genial, and good in bed. Sort of an idealized version of myself.

BAD BOBS I'VE KNOWN: Sadly, I know of a Bob I don't like, though happily I've never met him. An extraordinarily nasty person, he has even called his own mother dirty names in print. One of her biggest mistakes, clearly, was naming him Bob.

I'M HANDY AT...: I've just successfully reglued our car's rearview mirror to the windshield.

MOST IMPORTANT THING TO KNOW ABOUT WOMEN: Any man who imagines he can safely generalize about women is either insensitive or inexperienced.

TIME ON MY HAIR/MY LOOK: The Albert Einstein/Mark Twain look.

COMFORTWEAR: At night, pajamas.

BOYHOOD DREAM: To draw a science fiction comic strip.

FREE ADVICE: Try to work at something that gives you joy, regardless of what it pays or how much prestige is attached.

BOOK: *Bonfire of the Vanities*.

MOVIE: *Lawrence of Arabia*.

MAGAZINE: *Isaac Asimov's Science Fiction Magazine*.

CAR: Plymouth Voyager.

SONG: "A Day in the Life."

Bob Sirott, TV news anchor, Chicago, Illinois

WHAT BEING BOB MEANS: To be Bob is to be the monosyllabic fiber of Norman Rockwell's America.

MY GREAT WEEKEND: Getting the newspaper under the cat's head just in time to catch his throw-up.

BAD BOBS I'VE KNOWN: All Bobs are boring simpletons. I, like most Bobs, believe I am the one exception.

BEHAVIOR I DISLIKE: Symptoms of Tourette's syndrome.

MY HELL ON EARTH: Life without the missus.

MOST IMPORTANT THING TO KNOW ABOUT WOMEN: They are right all the time.

ON MY NIGHTSTAND: TV remote, wireless headphone remote, VCR remote.

TIME ON MY HAIR/MY LOOK: Half hour/the look of having more hair as I get older.

COMFORTWEAR: Baseball uniforms.

BOYHOOD DREAM: To be a radio announcer.

BOOK: *The Stranger* by Camus.

TV SHOW: *Whirlybirds*.

NEWS ANCHOR: John Chancellor.

SONG: "Spanish Harlem," by Ben E. King.

DRINK: Chocolate phosphate.

Bob Stupak, owner, Bob Stupak's Vegas World Hotel and Casino, Las Vegas, Nevada
WHY I'M BOB: I liked it.
WHAT BEING BOB MEANS: Simplicity.
MY GREAT WEEKEND: Winning at gambling and the companionship of a woman.
BAD BOBS I'VE KNOWN: Myself, sometimes.
I'M HANDY AT...: Massages.
BEHAVIOR I DISLIKE: Erratic.
MY HELL ON EARTH: Dealing with ex-wives.
WHO I TRUST AND DISTRUST: I trust my immediate family and no one else.
MOST IMPORTANT THING TO KNOW ABOUT WOMEN: How to handle them.
ON MY NIGHTSTAND: An ashtray and telephone.
TIME ON MY HAIR/MY LOOK: Fifteen minutes/Boyish.
BOYHOOD DREAM: To be a great movie actor.
FREE ADVICE: Never trust anyone but your mom and dad.
BOOK: *The Dreammakers* by Harold Robbins.

MOVIE: *Superman* and *Rocky*.
TV SHOW: Old *Twilight Zones*.
MAGAZINE: *Time* and *Newsweek*.
CEREAL: Rice Krispies.
CAR: Limo.
SONG: "Somewhere in Time."
AFTER-SHAVE: English Leather.
SPORT: Poker.
SANDWICH: Club.
DRINK: Gin and tonic wth a twist of lime.
NEWS ANCHOR: Walter Cronkite.
SMOKE: Carlton.

Bob Thomas, Hollywood columnist, Associated Press, Encino, California
WHY I'M BOB: When I started with AP at age 21, bylines were stodgy and I was billed as Robert J. Thomas. When I was assigned a Hollywood column at age 22, the bureau chief figured Robert J. Thomas was too formal for a guy who was going to interview starlets.
WHAT BEING BOB MEANS: Nothing. But it's a verb, and an active one at that. My wife is a verb too: Pat.
MY GREAT WEEKEND: To go body surfing.
I'M HANDY AT...: I'm all thumbs except at my typewriter and word processor. Sometimes there too.
BEHAVIOR I DISLIKE: Drunkenness.
MY HELL ON EARTH: A nine-to-five office job.
MOST IMPORTANT THING TO KNOW ABOUT WOMEN: That you'll never understand them.
ON MY NIGHTSTAND: A magazine with which to read my wife to sleep.
MOVIE: *Citizen Kane*.
TV SHOW: *Omnibus*.
MAGAZINE: *Vanity Fair* 1930.
SONG: "September Song."
AFTER-SHAVE: Never.
SANDWICH: Quesadilla.
DRINK: Champagne.

Bob Welch, musician, Mesa, Arizona
WHAT BEING BOB MEANS: I've been fighting Bob Blandness all my life, trying not to be too regular of a guy.
MOST IMPORTANT THINGS TO KNOW ABOUT WOMEN: That sex is not the most important thing to them; yet every woman, no matter how competent, likes to be considered and told that she's desirable.
ON MY NIGHTSTAND: Notes for songs written on napkins and beer coasters.

BOOK: *The Magus.*
CEREAL: Raisin Bran.
SONG: "Jump" by Van Halen.
DRINK: Bloody Mary.

Robert "Bob" Anton Wilson, science fiction author, Los Angeles, California

WHY I'M BOB: I use Bob for all purposes except book jackets. Bob Wilson is too common; in fact, the fourth most common name in America. But Robert Anton Wilson is remembered.
BAD BOBS I'VE KNOWN: Bob Shelton, imperial wizard of the KKK, a man too easy to predict.
MY HELL ON EARTH: A Marxist ecological, puritan democracy. (I currently see the world as a horde of zombies and a few wide-awake men and women.)
MOST IMPORTANT THINGS TO KNOW ABOUT WOMEN: They're nicer than men (kinder, gentler, etc.) except the feminists. They're nicer in bed too.
FREE ADVICE: A little pot won't hurt you, but stay away from cocaine.
BOOK: *Finnegan's Wake* by Joyce.
MOVIE: *Intolerance* (Griffith) and *The Trial* (Welles).
TV SHOW: *Hill Street Blues.*
MAGAZINE: *Utne Reader.*
SONG: "Greensleeves."
DRINK: Martini.

Bob Wolf, ad agency CEO (Chiat/Day/Mojo), Venice, California

WHY I'M BOB: I use Robert as my formal name and sign my name that way, but I never consider myself, informally, as Robert. I never considered Rob or Robby, either—too *My Three Sons.*
WHAT BEING BOB MEANS: Contemporary but not faddish; always appropriate.
I'M HANDY AT...: Finding handy people in the Yellow Pages.
MY HELL ON EARTH: An inescapable evening with boring people.
MOST IMPORTANT THINGS TO KNOW ABOUT WOMEN: Their core values, their sensual preferences, what car they drive.
ON MY NIGHTSTAND: Lamp, clock, magazines.
BOYHOOD DREAM: 4–6 years old, to be a cowboy; 7–8, a garbage man; 9–16, a pro athlete.
FREE ADVICE: Kids can do anything if they try their best. They should always be honest with themselves and with others.
BOOK: *The Making of the President 1960.*
TV SHOW: *L.A. Law.*
MAGAZINE: *Fortune* and *Vanity Fair.*
SPORT: Golf.
DRINK: Vodka and grapefruit juice.
NEWS ANCHOR: Cronkite.
SMOKE: Marlboro, but I gave it up.

PART FOUR:
THE BOB APPENDIX

AFTERWORD AND ACKNOWLEDGMENTS

No Bob could have written this book. No Bob would have thought of this book. Over the last four years we have been asked, not without good reason, why *we* did. Why would two guys *not* named Bob embark upon a sociology of guys *named* Bob? The answer is simple: Bob is okay. Little else in this world seems to be *as* okay as Bob. And Bob is everywhere. One of us had this epiphany the night he pulled into the parking lot of SmorgaBob's, a Bay area off-ramp eatery. He had the meat loaf and a vision. The other of us had spent his life closely observing the habits of a Bob—indeed, the Bob who spawned him. We both knew that in a culture corrupted by trendiness (and trend books), nothing could be less trendy than Bob. So, we decided to start a new trend—an anti-trend, really. And that would be Bob. Bob: The Death of Trends.

Bobs are unaccustomed to being acknowledged, much less celebrated. It took more than two celebrants to bring this project to life. We now acknowledge those who acknowledged Bob when it counted. From the beginning, there was Jody Rein, an editor of remarkable foresight, insight, and patience, who understood Bob, in a word. We said "Bob." She said, "Of course." Madeleine Morel persevered, just like a Bob, in our behalf, and aggressively cheered us on. Ivy Brown scoured landscape and library for Bobs; her bright editorial detective work sustained our enthusiasm and earned our unflinching gratitude. Cindy Price found Bobs where few would have dared to look, compiled the startling Bob statistics, and inspired us with her unwavering Bob faith. Charles Hamilton was the picture of tenacity in his hunt for Bob pictures. Kay Schuckhart knows what Bob looks like and gave *The Bob Book* its Bob-like look. And special thanks go to Bob Greene, who we hope will now *enjoy* being a Bob; and to Bob Mankoff, who gave face and heart, in illustration, to Bob.

Bobs give credit where credit is due, and in that spirit, we thank, in alphabetical order, the following people for their encouragement, help and tolerance. If we've forgotten anyone, you know who you are and you know it's simply an oversight at the end of a long, long road: Bill and Betsy Archer; Bob Atwan; Jane Ayer; Steven Baker; Tracy Barone; John Baeder; Stephanie Bennett and Jim Mervis; Sandra Bernhard; The Bobs; Howard Bragman; David Burke; Michael and Cynthia Chaney; Marcia Froelke Coburn, who knows everything; Bob Crane, Jr.; Cameron Crowe; Bob Cummings, for being the first; Julia Daly; Peter de Jonghe; Bob ("You guys are so full of shit") Eubanks; Ian Frazier; D.G. Fulford; Bob Gale and Mary Anne DeSimone; Bob Garfield; G. Barry Golson; Ward Grant at Hope Enterprises; Kathy Greco; Tammy Haddad; Phyllis Halliday; Penny Lee Hallin; David Handelman; Larry Henry; Clarkson Hine; Mike Howard; Bob Hope, for being the best; Jennifer Howe; Richard Hull and Donna Tadelman; Cheryl Boone Isaacs; Genelle Izumi-Uyekawa; Garrison Keillor; Larry King; Mary Jo Kinser; Dennis Klein; Judd Klinger; KROQ's Laura Brown and Kevin & Bean; Lady, Louise and Louie, Jr.; Bob the Cat; Gary Larson; Kelly Leisten; Mike Lintner at Jim Beam; John McAlley; John McVie; Bob Mackie; Bob Manley; Jody and Allan Marcil; Garry Meier; Ellen Meloy; Jing Mercado; Bob Miller; Susan Morrison; John Newsom; Jarl Olsen and Bob Barrie; Kathy O'Malley; Sandy O'Neill; Christopher Pallotto D.D.S.; Bob Payton; Tiff Payne at Karseal; The Peterson Family and Apryl; Neal and Kimberly Preston; Steve Randall; Ernest and Gerda Rensin (with love), who got it; the Joe Rensin family; John Rezek; Bernadette Sabath; Kendra Saddler; Vidal Sassoon; Bob Shea; Bob Sirott and Carrie Cochran; Bob Smith at Simi Valley Software; Loni Specter; Francine and Ed Stasium, for tea and sympathy; Peter Travers; Bob Wallace; Richard C. Woods; Bob Woodward; Bob and Suzanne Zehme, for being the prototypical Bob & Wife; and Christina Zimmel, who made a damn fine lunch. Of course, we profoundly thank the Bobs who responded to The Bob Survey, for sharing.

And, with enduring love from her father, for Lucy Ellen.

If you're compelled to write to *The Bob Book*, here's the address: THE BOB BOOK, Box 55301, Sherman Oaks, CA 91413.

CREDIT WHERE CREDIT IS DUE

Excerpt from Bob Tway profile "The Golfing Machine," reprinted courtesy of the author.
Dinosaur Bob: Reproduced from *Dinosaur Bob and His Adventures with the Family Lazardo*, by William Joyce. Copyright © 1988 by William Joyce. Published by Harper & Row, Publishers, Inc. Reprinted by permission.
Bob's Books are published by Price, Stern, Sloan, Los Angeles, CA. Copyright © 1989 by Bob McGrath.
Bob "Meaning of Life"
Recycled Paper Products, Inc., All Rights Reserved.
Original Design by Forrest Pasky, Reprinted by permission.
Bob Richards with the Wheaties Box: Used with the permission of Bob Richards and General Mills, Inc.
Bob Toothgrinder: Reprinted courtesy of Kevin Pope, artist.
Big Boy Bop: Reprinted courtesy of John Baeder and OK Harris Gallery.
The Book of the Subgenius cover reprinted by permission of Simon & Schuster, Inc. (Fireside Books)
Bob's Self-Improvement Seminar: Designed by Bradco Graphics.
Bobbing for Fun (three game-show hosts) ad and photo of Bob Newhart "Bob in Lights" : Reprinted by permission of CBS Television and the artists.
Photo of Bob Restaurant at the Taj Mahal, by David Handelman.
Bob's Biggest Fears postcard courtesy of John Rodgers, ArtBoy of Chicago.
Bob Uecker: Both excerpts from *Playboy*'s 20 Questions. Copyright 1987 by *Playboy*.
Letter from Montana: by Ellen Meloy. First appeared in *Wigwag* magazine, reprinted courtesy of *Wigwag* and Ellen Meloy.
Bob Across America photos: courtesy of Bob Manley.
Bob Hope Photos: courtesy Bob Hope Collection.
Photo of Bob Hope/Bob Eubanks, courtesy NBC.
Bob Traffic Signs courtesy of Nissan and Chiat/Day/Mojo
Photo of *Twin Peaks*' Bob ("The embodiment of all evil in the world") courtesy of Lynch/Frost Productions
Photos of Bob's Big Boy courtesy of Marriott Family Restaurants
"Get Laid" greeting card art courtesy of Nobleworks
Hurricane Chart courtesy of the National Weather Service
Bob Cummings photos: courtesy Bob Cummings Collection.
Photos of Robert Goulet (ladder and wedding), Bobby Knight, Bob Cratchit, Bob Feller 1956, Bob Cousy: Reprinted by permission of UPI/Bettman Newsphotos.
Photos of Bob Welch (pitcher), Bob Welch (musician), Bob Dylan, Bob Geldof, Bob Seger: by Neal Preston.
All Photos of Vidal Sassoon courtesy of Vidal Sassoon, Inc.

Photos of Dr. Bob courtesy of The Founders Foundation.
Photographs of Bobs Leary, the Elder and Younger, from the collection of Bob and Ellen Leary.
THE BOB BOOK logo was designed by David Rensin.
All other photos courtesy of the people pictured, their publicists, secretaries, managers, friends, acquaintances; *The Bob Book* photo research department and the authors' nagging persistence.

THE BOB INDEX

What follows are the names, ages, occupations, and residences of the Bobs whose Bob Survey responses found their way into *The Bob Book*. Their contributions—and the contributions of any survey respondents not collected here—are quietly appreciated, for this is the only way Bobs like appreciation shown. The numbers key each Bob to quoted responses listed throughout most of *The Bob Book*.

77. Geline, 43, Writer/TV Producer, New York, NY
78. Gershon, Tenafly, NJ
79. Gliha, 30, Lab Technician, Westlake, OH
80. Gordon, 46, Builder/Organic Herb Grower, Hammond Ranch, CA
81. Graf, 30, CAD Technician, Fond du Lac, WI
82. Grant, 20, Student, NY
83. Hansen, 27, Freelance Consultant, Milwaukee, WI
84. Hargrove, 47, Retired, San Antonio, TX
85. Hart, 19, Student, Syracuse, NY
86. Hilton, 39, Computer System Manager, Little Rock, AR
87. Hilton, 65, Instrumentation Engineer, Calgary, Alberta
88. Himes, 25, Emergency Services Dispatcher, Kodiak, AK
89. Hlavac, 33, Body Shop Manager, Palmdale, CA
90. Hogan, 34, Insurance Executive, Westlake Village, CA
91. Hopping, 22, Residential Appraiser Trainee, Fairfield, OH
92. Howard, 58, Maintenance Supervisor/Salesman, Creston, NC
93. Howley, 43, Interior Landscaper, Malibu, CA
94. Hull, Jr., 31, Janitor, Wheeling, WV
95. Iannacone, 25, Podiatrist, Garden City, NY
96. Jackson, 38, Learning Disabilities Consultant, Berlin, NJ
97. Jameson, 38, Sales Manager, Spring, TX
98. Jenkins, 29, La Mesa, CA
99. Johnson, 23, Milan, IL
100. Jones, 27, Student, Las Vegas, NV
101. Jones, 56, Salesman, Upland, CA
102. Jordan, 19, Student, Woodland, CA
103. Jordan, 24, Legal Assistant, Garden City, NY
104. Kanarick, 49, Marketing Manager, Pine Brook, NJ
105. Kanyer, 28, Salesman/Student, Seattle, WA
106. Kempf, 30, Actor, Los Angeles, CA
107. Kettinger, 47, Accountant, North Andover, MA
108. Kieta, 42, Regional Sales Manager, Palos Park, IL
109. Klinger, 43, Pediatrician, Westerville, OH
110. Kral, Jr., 30, Grocery Store Manager, OH
111. Kral, Sr., 56, Police Sergeant, OH
112. Kunkel, 47, Deputy Sheriff/Jail Administrator, Kimball, MN
113. Kurek, 23, Mechanic/Rigger, Chicago, IL
114. Larsen, 42, Fireman, Mission Hills, CA
115. Leary, 36, Merchant, Westmont, NJ
116. Lehr, 44, Word Processor/Student, San Francisco, CA
117. Levatino, 38, Accounting Manager, Holmdel, NJ
118. Lind, 56, Newspaper Writer, Fargo, ND
119. Little, 27, Athletic Director, Waltham, MA
120. Lofquist, 26, Counselor, Plainville, CT
121. Lonsdale, 68, Retired School Counselor, Sepulveda, CA
122. Lovell, 37, Advertising, Rockford, IL
123. Luetkenhaus, 21, Management Trainee, St. Charles, MO
124. Mair, 27, Accountant/Reggae Singer, New York, NY
125. Malcheski, Jr., 35, Paste-Up Artist/Caterer/Etc., Los Angeles, CA
126. Gibson, 50, Public Relations, Los Angeles, CA
127. Malone, 40, Office Worker, Chandler, AZ
128. Mangini, 53, Retired Construction Teamster, Kailua-Kona, HI
129. Manley, 25, Photographer, Hollywood, CA

130. Mark, 25, Food Manager, Santa Cruz, CA
131. Martin, Hair Salon Owner, Los Angeles, CA
132. Martin, 24, Machinist, Philadelphia, PA
133. Martin, 32, Trucker, Dallas, TX
134. McAuliff, 28, Construction Project Coordinator, Los Angeles, CA
135. Brown, Jr., 33, Sales-Termites, Dania, FL
136. McKaig, 39, Staff Engineer, Mechanicsville, VA
137. McKinzie, 25, Optical Lab Prod. Manager, Chula Vista, CA
138. McKinzie, 61, Truck Driver, Oklahoma City, OK
139. Medici, 34, Musician/Carpenter/Designer, New York, NY
140. Merlis, 41, Publicist, Los Angeles, CA
141. Milan, 25, Drummer, Chandler, AZ
142. Miller, 34, Editor, New York, NY
143. Misiti, 30, Executive Chef, Farmingdale, NY
144. Mook, 62, Roofing and Sheet Metal Contractor, Flossmoor, IL
145. Mooney, 35, Artist, Dallas, TX
146. Moreno, 32, Fire Sprinkler Fabricator, IN
147. Motto, 49, Field Service Engineer, Dallas, TX
148. Mound, 32, Chef, Madison, NJ
149. Munn, 37, General Manager, CA
150. Murray, 30, Movie Set Carpenter, Tucson, AZ
151. Myers, 67, Job Coach, Sepulveda, CA
152. Neal, 46, Process Server, Shawnee, OK
153. Nelson, 19, Student, Valparaiso, NE
154. Nelson, 40, College Professor, Waterville, ME
155. O'Brien, 20, Student, Eustis, FL
156. Pagani, 38, Radio Personality/Writer, Phillipsburg, NJ
157. Palme, 30, Machinist, Casco, ME
158. Parrish, 27, Project Manager, Mt. Holly, NJ
159. Pearson, 28, Painter, Bellevue, WA
160. Pett, 48, Sales Representative, Wanague, NJ
161. Phelps, 47, Newspaper Columnist, Jacksonville, FL
162. Polk, 37, Marketing Consultant, Clarkston, GA
163. Pond, 52, Real Estate Broker, Granada Hills, CA
165. Porlier, 46, Loss Prevention Investigator, Pasadena, CA
165. Posey, 44, Dealer Licensing, Columbus, OH
166. Proppe, 51, Antique Book Dealer, Arkadelphia, AR
167. Przybylski, 28, Video Producer/Director, Bay City, MI
168. Purcell, 65, Retired, Las Vegas, NV
169. Pyle, 43, Control Systems Consultant, Calgary, Alberta
170. Quade, College Professor, Hackettstown, NJ
171. Ralls, 47, Real Estate Manager, La Canada-Flintridge, CA
172. Rancourt, Jr., 20, Waiter, Alexandria, VA
173. Reich, 47, Army Officer, Ft. Gordon, GA
174. Reisse, 45, Electrical Engineer, Frankfort, IL
175. Renna, 45, Textile Cutter, Montrose, PA
176. Richerter, 35, Mr. Mom/Writer, Merrick, NY
177. Rochelle, 32, Restaurant Owner, Boone, NC
178. Ruth, 30, Real Estate Developer, Los Angeles, CA
179. Santee, 25, Optical Lab Supervisor, Columbus, OH
180. Schenkman, 52, CPA, Encino, CA
181. Schneider, 31, Sewing Manufacturer/Musician, Shelbyville, IN
182. Scott, 27, Paramedic Supervisor, Oxnard, CA
183. Shaw, 59, Aircraft Structure Mechanic, Van Nuys, CA
184. Sidell, 52, Make-up Artist, Chatsworth, CA

185. Sipchen, 36, Writer/Reporter, Los Angeles, CA
186. Smith, 24, Navy Nuclear Engineer, WA
187. Smith, 34, Computer Store Owner, Canoga Park, CA
188. Smith, 41, Salesman, W. Orange, NJ
189. Smith, 38, Teacher, Charlotte, MI
190. Sotomayo, Jr., 31, Traffic Manager, Whittier, CA
191. Spatz, 44, Counselor, Deerfield, IL
192. Spencer, 34, Casino Slot Manager, Sparks, NV
193. Storm, 20, Air Crew Life-Support Specialist, USAF, APO, NY
194. Stroud, 38, Disc Jockey, Chicago, IL
195. Taylor, 60, Iron Worker, Ft. Wayne, IN
196. The Unknown Bob, pencil on green paper
197. Thell, 26, Sales Representative, Dayton, OH
198. Thompson, 32, Fire Protection Designer, Pt. St. Lucie, FL
199. Turley, Retired New York Yankees Pitcher, Marco Island, FL
200. Urban, 28, Chef, Wilkes-Barre, PA
201. Vande Velde, 64, Distributing Company Owner, IA
202. Vane, 34, Paralegal, Santa Margarita, CA
203. Vasilopulos, 31, Sports Producer, Chicago, IL
204. Villines, 56, Teacher, Tarzana, CA
205. Vranicar, 33, Systems Analyst
206. Ward, 54, Writer, Austin, TX
207. Wdowiak, 48, Legal Secretary, San Francisco, CA
208. Weis, 32, Executive Producer, Glendale, CA
209. Weisman, Jr., 20, Student, Monaca, PA
210. Williams, 40, Sales Manager, Indianapolis, IN
211. Winningham, 28, Human Resources Analyst, Camarillo, CA
212. Wiren, 40, Hairdresser, Englewood, NJ
213. Wolff, 35, Water Plant Operator, Princeton, IL
214. Wood, Jr., 47, High School Latin Teacher, Arcade, NY
215. Woolf, 62, Sports and Entertainment Attorney, Boston, MA
216. Wright, 18, Student, Akron, OH
217. Wright, 42, English Teacher, Staten Island, NY
218. Young, 41, Teacher, Glendale, CA
219. Zamites, 25, Student, Santa Fe, NM

When A Bob is Not A Bob

- Bobolink: A North American singing bird, also called a rice bird.
- Bobsled: A sled made of two short sleds coupled together. Used in drawing Logs.
- Bobtail: The tail of a horse cut short.
- Bobwhite: The common partridge of North America.
- Bob-a-day: Temporary gunnery officer.
- Bobanob: A shilling per head.
- Bob and sock: Boxing.
- Bob around: To go quickly from place to place (shift one's bob).
- Bob cull: A good fellow or pleasant companion.
- Bob-down man: an antiaircraft sentry. His warning caused men to take cover.
- Bob down—you're spotted!: You're argument is so very weak that you need not go on.
- Bob groin: A racehorse betting ring.
- Bob hole door: A wagon door constructed to half open so that an employee may bob in or out.
- Bob Hope: A flying bomb, circa 1944. "When you hear them coming, you bob, hope for the best."
- Bob Squash: To wash oneself. Hence the lavatory division of a public convenience.
- Bob's-a-dying: Idling and dozing (nautical usage).
- Bobs' Own: An early nickname of the Irish Guards raised in 1900, from their first Colonel, Lord Roberts.
- Bob's your uncle: Everything is all right. "There, I've done it."

"Face it, if Bob can write a book, anyone can." —JERRY ROBINSON, orthodontist, on his friend Dr. Bob Hartley

eeeeeeeeeeeeeee

ATTENTION, BOBS!

Your Bob perspectives are welcome for inclusion in special, future Bob projects. If you're inclined to participate, we urge you to complete this new, abridged Bob survey, at your earliest convenience.

THE NEW BOB SURVEY

Name:
Address:
City/State/Zip:
Phone:
Occupation:
Age:

CLASSIC BOB QUESTIONS

1. Why did you stick with the name Bob, instead of Robert, Bobby, Robby, Rob, etc.?

2. What does it mean to be Bob?

BOB'S WORLD QUESTIONS

3. When do you feel most accomplished, and describe the feeling.

4. What's your version of hell on earth?

5. What's your secret to looking good? Your style tips?

6. What should the woman in your life know about you from the start?

7. What are the most important things to know about women? Describe the perfect wife.

8. What should every father know? [Fathers only, please!]

9. What possessions should no man be without?

10. What's the best way to stay sane in an insane world?

11. What's your life philosophy?

Please send to: THE BOB BOOK Box 55301 Sherman Oaks, CA. 91413